ELEMENTS OF ANTHROPOLOGY
*A Series of Introductions*

# American Culture: An Anthropological Perspective

## Lucy R. Garretson

Temple University

WM. C. BROWN COMPANY PUBLISHERS
Dubuque, Iowa

**ANTHROPOLOGY SERIES**
Consulting Editors

*Frank Johnston*
*University of Pennsylvania*

*Henry Selby*
*Temple University*

Printed in the United States of America

# *Contents*

Introduction   v

1   Nature, Rationality, and the American Dream   1

2   Home, School and Work: Learning to Be American   14

3   Variations on American Themes   27

4   Dream and Reality   47

Glossary   54

Index   57

For Mary Kerr Garretson

# Introduction

This book will present an introduction to American culture from an anthropological point of view. Traditionally, anthropology involves fieldwork, a period of time spent living with the "natives," participating in their daily lives, and asking questions about what they do and believe. By the end of the fieldwork period, the anthropologist usually will be acquainted with most of the people in the village or the tribe being studied. When an account of the culture of the people is written up, the anthropologist tries to give a complete and well-rounded picture, showing the relationships among all aspects of the social system, including religion, marriage customs, myth, economics, warfare, and so on. The aim is to present the culture as an integrated whole.

Ideally, an introduction to American culture should also give the reader a complete and well-rounded picture, based on fieldwork, data collection, and participant observation. Yet there are some difficulties in studying American culture which make the attempt unlike that of the ordinary anthropological study of a whole society.

First, there are over 200 million Americans; they are not all alike, and they don't all live in the same place. No anthropologist could know firsthand even a small percentage of this population. Second, Americans are literate. They write histories, economics textbooks, psychoanalyses, novels, and television serials about themselves. They also count themselves and publish censuses.

They tabulate the numbers of people who work in factories and on farms. They publish statistics on steel production and the number of dog licenses issued. So even though I am a "native," I cannot know all there is to know about America. What then could I tell an outsider, one who has no knowledge of the culture, about America?

I could begin by reciting facts, such as, the average American family has 2.4 children. Or I could amaze a visitor by giving statistics on the number of yards of paper towels produced and used by Americans. However, an outsider would probably dismiss the first statistic as meaningless: how could anyone have four-tenths of a child? And while guesses about the level of technology required to make paper towels could be made, such facts presented in isolation would not give much insight into American life. The visitor would have to know something about the American belief in personal cleanliness and in the germ theory of disease. The fact that paper towels are thrown away might lead to the inference that Americans believe in unending abundance and conspicuous consumption. In other words, the visitor would want to learn *why* paper towels are produced and used by Americans. In order to find the answer to that question, he or she would have to learn as much as possible about America, about the meaning of shared customs, beliefs, and symbols to Americans.

# AMERICAN CULTURE: AN ANTHROPOLOGICAL PERSPECTIVE
## Introduction

One American symbol, for instance, is the flag. The American flag is a rectangular piece of material, made up of bits of red, white, and blue colored cloth, cut and sewn into a particular design. A visitor could observe that Americans act in certain ways when they see the flag. American school children often begin the school day by placing their right hands over their hearts and reciting a memorized "pledge of allegiance." When the flag passes in a parade, Americans salute it, bringing their right hands up to their foreheads. The visitor could notice that Americans do not perform these actions when they see other kinds of flags, or other rectangular pieces of cloth, and conclude that the American flag has a special meaning for Americans. The next step would be to discover what this meaning is, and here a visitor might become confused. Some Americans might be observed burning the flag and might state that they were expressing *opposition* to governmental policies. But other Americans might be seen pasting the flag on their car windows and might explain that they were expressing *support* for governmental policies. Our visitor might conclude that whether Americans burn the flag or salute it, the flag evokes emotion. It carries complex meanings which are not explainable by describing its colors or design. In other words, the flag is a *symbol* for Americans. Further, Americans share the knowledge that the flag has a meaning, although they may interpret this knowledge differently and may act differently in regard to the flag.

Our visitor would now have begun to learn something about one bit of American *culture*. Culture is defined here as the *learned set of shared beliefs and shared understandings about the meaning of symbols*. Because, like the symbol of the flag, there are many other shared symbols and beliefs in America, we can describe American culture by outlining these beliefs and the ways in which beliefs and actions are interrelated. The fact that certain beliefs are shared and understood by Americans does not mean, of course, that all Americans act the same way. But Americans do learn, as part of a school textbook lesson or as part of the general process of growing up in America, a set of assumptions and beliefs about the world, their country, and themselves. By looking at these assumptions, we can hope to present a picture of American culture as a whole. How are American beliefs concerning democracy, for instance, related to American beliefs about family structure, personal prestige, or education? The following chapters will serve as a primer, for the interested outsider and for Americans, to introduce the principles of American culture.

These principles will be presented as basic ideas in chapter 1. In the first part of the chapter we will deal with the historical influences affecting the way in which nature, rationality, and culture are related in American thought. The second part of chapter 1 will look at the "American Dream" and at some of the implications of this expression of American ideals. In chapter 2, we will see how the kind of thinking that underlies the American Dream is related to American cultural beliefs about the family and the school, where children learn "how to be an American" and how these worlds of home and school are connected to the adult world of work.

In chapter 3, we will turn from the world of ideals and beliefs to the everyday world; we will look at some studies of actual groups of Americans. Finally, in chapter 4, we will look at some of the ways in which statements like "all men are created equal" conflict with the fact of social inequality in American society. We will try to explain why in American culture, as in others, beliefs and symbols may seem to be far removed from reality and yet may continue to constitute an underlying cultural order.

# 1 | Nature, Rationality, and the American Dream

In assessing the origins of the United States we begin by looking at the Declaration of Independence and the Constitution, documents which established the nation, and at the kinds of beliefs that led to the writing of these documents. Unlike anthropologists who work with nonliterate peoples, we have a written record which we can consult to explain the historical roots of culture, as well as an archeological record from which we can learn about the more remote past. In this case the written documents have primary importance, since we are dealing with American culture rather than with the history of the peoples who have inhabited the continent of North America. Although the United States today is a much bigger country, contains a much larger population, and is technologically much more sophisticated than the original coalition of thirteen colonies in the eighteenth century, Americans still speak of the writers of the Declaration of Independence and the Constitution as "Founding Fathers." Although some provisions of the Constitution have been changed by amendment, the original system of government remains in force. Further, the ideological underpinnings—the assumptions that guided the thinking of the Founding Fathers—may still be found to underlie much of American culture today. Therefore it is appropriate to begin a discussion of the American belief system with a brief look at the history of the founding of the nation.

## HISTORICAL INFLUENCES

Anthropologists agree that the species *Homo sapiens* did not originate in the New World. The earliest dated human bones found in America are those of Midland Man (actually a skeleton of a woman), thought to be at least 10,000 years old. Human beings probably entered the New World by crossing a land bridge over the Bering Strait, perhaps between thirty-five and fifty thousand years ago. The descendants of these immigrants from Asia were called "Indians" by the early European explorers.

Over the centuries, the Indians had developed distinct cultures. It has been estimated that there were more than 200 mutually unintelligible languages spoken by native peoples north of Mexico at the time the white man came. There was an equal diversity of cultural practices and differences in physical appearance among the tribes, who felt themselves to be distinct and unique, much as later German immigrants felt themselves dissimilar to the Irish. In the seventeenth and eighteenth centuries, some merging of tribes into bigger political units occurred, the League of the Iroquois

1

being the most notable example, but the various tribes had not in general attempted any large-scale political consolidation. But though the form of political organization which was to become the United States of America was largely a creation of European immigrants, we can trace some Indian influence on its structure. Benjamin Franklin, for one, was said to have been much impressed with the structure of the League of the Iroquois. The creation of two houses in the U.S. Congress was influenced by the Iroquois division of *sachems* and *pine trees* as well as by the British model of the House of Lords and the House of Commons. Further, Senate and House committees work out bills in compromise session in ways similar to those used by the Iroquois League.[1]

In a philosophical sense the discovery of other human beings in the New World also had an indirect effect on the thinking of the men who framed the Declaration of Independence and the Constitution. Early European explorers had written of the "noble savage." They had been impressed by the dignity, freedom, and simplicity of the Indian way of life. Their accounts were widely read in Europe and led some thinkers to believe that in the state of nature human beings are naturally happy and free, and to conclude that it is the institution of government which tyrannizes and brutalizes. Although accounts of the "happy noble savage" were based on misconceptions about both the simplicity and the savagery of the native Americans, the vision of a Utopian wilderness out of which human beings could forge their own identity and choose their own form of government helped inspire rebellion in the British colonies.

Other influences on the thinking of the Founding Fathers can be traced to the intellectual climate of eighteenth century Europe, particularly England. The men who framed the United States government were, almost to a man, of British descent. Many of them were lawyers, schooled in British

common law. They were products of the period of intellectual history called the Enlightenment—they believed in the rationality of man. They felt reason would lead eventually to the discovery of "the Laws of Nature and of Nature's God," a phrase used in the first sentence of the Declaration of Independence. The eighteenth century signaled the rise of the scientific method, along with the rejection of magical and mystical thinking. "Nature's God," himself, was believed by many men to be rather remote from the daily affairs of humans. His laws, like the laws of motion, could be understood by rational human beings. God was thought to be rather like a great clockmaker.

The removal of the realm of the sacred from everyday life led also to the rejection of temporal authority. As Louis Dumont points out, in traditional societies social differences between groups of humans are accepted as being part of a natural and sacred order. For instance, medieval European thinkers had expressed this idea by the phrase, "the great chain of being." This chain was believed to be an enduring ordering of all living things—animals at the bottom, humans in between, and God at the top. Social differences were therefore considered sacred because it was "ordained" by God that some humans ranked higher in the chain than others. By contrast, the eighteenth century emphasis on human rationality implied that the individual is the important unit (rather than a social class or a social institution like the monarchy) because it is the individual—not a group or institution—who *thinks*. Dumont argues, then, that principles of equality are the logical outcome of an ideology which emphasizes individual rationality, since the most simple assumption that can be made is that *all* individuals are rational and therefore in

1. Alvin M. Josephy, Jr., *The Indian Heritage of America* (New York: Bantam Books, 1969), p. 34.

that respect equal.[2] The assumption that individuals are inherently equal also clearly negates the principles upon which acceptance of social inequalities rested. Thus in embracing the principle of individual rationality, the American colonists rejected the doctrine that the British King could do no wrong and that the king's power ultimately was God-given. The person of the monarch and the rule of the state were no longer considered sacred. Therefore rational men could and should consider whether the policy of government was directed to the interest of the citizens. The divine right of kings was replaced in the Constitution with the rights of the people. The words of the Preamble of the Constitution read, "We, the People of the United States . . . do ordain and establish this Constitution for the United States of America."

At the time, the establishment of the American democracy was viewed as a radical experiment. The new government did not include a monarch nor, specifically, a privileged governing class like the European nobility. Instead, the Americans argued that "all men are created equal"; that all men have a claim to rationality and to participation in self-government. However, the inherent equality of men and their right to establish their own form of government did not imply, to these eighteenth century writers, that law and order should be abandoned in favor of anarchy. On the contrary, the American government was established with a written Constitution, which remains the law of the land today. The framers of the Constitution did not argue for a return to a (mythical) savage state of complete freedom. They felt that while all men may be created equal, all men will remain unenlightened (like "savages") unless they use their powers of reason, and unless they organize themselves in orderly fashion under the law—the product of the use of human reason.

Further, they argued that since human beings are by *nature* rational (thus different from animals) human laws are also *natural,* part of true human nature. Anarchy, or complete lawlessness, would be like the law of the jungle and would be nonhuman and wrong. But government established by "the people" and with their consent consists of human-made laws which are morally right. In American culture it is therefore the Constitution which enables Americans to make the transition from the state of anarchy—that is, the state of nature—to the state of lawful government—that is, the state of culture.

The U.S. Constitution, then, is both an actual document and a symbol. It is a pivot which transforms unorganized human nature, through rationality, into moral human society. This kind of relationship between nature and culture, in particular the role of rationality in transforming nature into human culture, can be seen at many levels of the American belief system.[3] A shorthand way of presenting this complex idea can be introduced by setting up a key sentence: "Nature transformed by rationality results in culture." In this sentence, "nature," "rationality," and "culture" can take on different specific definitions, depending on what subject we are talking about. Thus the form of the sentence can be used to express ideas about various aspects of American culture. In the following diagram the variant of the original sentence that expresses the idea we have been discussing is included—that the Constitution of the United States effects the transformation, on a governmental level, from nature to culture. Later on we will add

2. Louis Dumont, *Homo Hierarchicus* (Chicago: University of Chicago Press, 1970), p. 253.

3. I am indebted to David Schneider for suggesting this relationship between culture and nature in American culture in his discussion of marriage and the family in *American Kinship: A Cultural Account* (Englewood Cliffs, N.J.: Prentice-Hall, 1968). I have expanded and undoubtedly distorted his original notion.

substitute terms in each of the three slots to organize other aspects of American culture in accordance with this general plan.

We can recognize that implicit in this scheme is the judgment that "culture," because it is the product of reason, is *morally better* than "nature." For instance, although few Americans read the Constitution or in fact are well informed about its provisions, they believe in its sanctity. A law or a political act which is judged "constitutional" is accepted as morally right, while "unconstitutional" laws and actions are struck down. The authority of the Constitution may even be invoked in order to censure the highest elected government official, the president of the United States, if his actions are judged unconstitutional.

Americans also assume that since their form of government is rational and moral, it is therefore superior to other kinds of governments. The belief in the innate good of American democracy has been used to justify both expansionist and colonial policies. For instance, in regard to the geographic expansion of American territory, the nineteenth century phrase "manifest destiny" indicated that the westward movement to the Pacific Ocean was both inevitable and morally correct. Similarly, Americans have almost always believed, at least until the unpopular wars in Southeast Asia, that American economic or military intervention in the affairs of another nation was justified because the American form of government was basically good. The attempt by the U.S. Central Intelligence Agency to overthrow the government of Cuba at the Bay of Pigs was considered a scandal mostly because it failed. If it had succeeded in "throwing out the Communists," most Americans would have approved because they believe as a matter of faith that communistic governments are morally inferior to their own.

The sanctity of established government under law is well established. Few Americans, even though they may desire far-reaching changes in the laws, would advocate scrapping the Constitution and starting all over again. This belief goes hand-in-hand with the doctrine of individual responsibility for action implied by a belief in equality. If all humans are equal and rational, then all individuals must account for themselves. When governmental functions appear to be inadequate or wrong, the institution of government is not questioned, but, rather, the individual person in government is liable to be criticized. For instance, the Watergate scandals of 1973-74 elicited many calls for the removal of the president but few demands for the abolishment of the office of the presidency. Like the flag, the "office of the President of the United States" is symbolic of the United States itself. However, Amer-

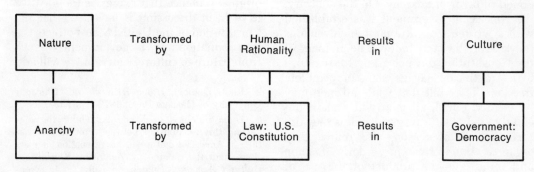

**FIGURE 1.1**
THE ROLE OF THE CONSTITUTION

icans can and do judge the individual occupant of that office personally. They may respect the position while despising the president.

## THE LAND: INDIVIDUALISM AND ABUNDANCE

The emphasis on individual responsibility relates, as already said, to the intellectual and moral climate of eighteenth-century Europe. But the extreme form of individualism espoused by Americans also has other roots, more closely traceable to the New World itself—to the land. The territory which was to become the United States of America was vast and relatively unpopulated. Most European immigrants saw the indigenous peoples either as "savages" or "children" and therefore not a population of human beings. The Indian tribes were usually viewed as one more natural obstacle to be overcome in "conquering" the land. The vast, "unpopulated" land also was rich in resources. Although in the early years of European settlement a fur trade flourished, the chief resource was the land itself, luring explorers and settlers westward. In 1763 the king of England issued a proclamation forbidding settlements further inland than the sources of rivers flowing into the Atlantic Ocean, but it was already too late to stop by fiat the westward flow. The boundless land provided opportunities lacking in more settled parts of the world and attracted the European peasantry.

The people who chose to move westward in the seventeenth and eighteenth centuries found themselves isolated from European influence and civilization. They were forced to become self-reliant and independent, as the Puritans of the Massachusetts Bay Colony had been. Throughout the nineteenth century, the frontier continued to exist, and people who lived on it lived a life of independence to survive. In 1894, four years after the U.S. Census Bureau officially proclaimed the end of the frontier, Frederick Jackson Turner argued that the frontier itself had created what was uniquely American in the character of the United States. The frontier, he said, promoted a disdain of "soft" civilization and the settled elites of the Eastern seaboard because the hardships of frontier life applied equally to all who dared face them. Turner felt that status differences on the frontier were erased and that in facing the hardships of frontier life, the "true" American was created. Differences stemming from European backgrounds disappeared as did the sense of being "British." Further, he insisted that pioneers forced to rely on themselves and their families, became contemptuous of any other authority. Having survived the hostility of nature by themselves, they developed a feeling that nobody could or should tell them what was right to do. Therefore he traced the American indifference to or dislike of politicians, politics, and centralization of governmental functions directly to the frontier influence.[4] Turner thus isolated one influence which adds to the American creed of individualism and belief in independent equality. He stressed the Americanization, liberation, and fusion of immigrants, but he overlooked another important factor which also plays a large part in the American belief system, namely, that the expansion of the population westward resulted also in the creation of abundant material goods. Here we touch on another important American characteristic.

Even as they rejected anarchy and sought to frame a rational government under law, so did the pioneers feel that the wilderness, though beautiful and abundant, should be tamed. The savage state was not seen as ideal here either. Land was meant to be

4. Frederick Jackson Turner, "The Significance of the Frontier in American History," in *An American Primer,* ed. Daniel J. Boorstin (Chicago: The University of Chicago Press, 1966), pp. 524-27.

used, to be farmed in order that it might produce. In 1705, years before the American Revolution, Robert Beverly, a Virginia planter, wrote that while the territory of Virginia was one of the "gardens of the world," there were too few gardens in Virginia. As Leo Marx explains, when Beverly speaks of Virginia as one of the "gardens of the world," he is using the language of myth:

Here the garden stands for the original unity, the all-sufficing beauty and abundance of the creation. Virginia is an Edenic land of primitive splendor inhabited by noble savages.

But when Beverly says that there are too few gardens in Virginia, he is speaking about actual, man-made, cultivated pieces of ground. This image is an emblem of abundance, but it refers to abundance produced by work, or, in Beverly's idiom, improvement.[5]

Nature uncontrolled was meant to be overcome through human rationality—through the application of science and technology—and thus made cultural. As technological advances were made through the years, they were logically used to extract from the land what it would yield. David M. Potter writes:

The factor of abundance, which we first discovered as an environmental condition and which we then converted into a cultural as well as a physical force, has not only influenced all the aspects of American life in a fundamental way but has also impinged upon our relations with the peoples of the world, and our failure to realize the nature of the relationship between this abundance and our democracy has played a critical part in frustrating our attempts to fulfill the mission of America.[6]

In addition, Potter says that the American exploitation of resources is also unique to Americans, that:

Abundance resides in a series of physical potentialities which have never been inventoried at the same value for any two cultures in the past and are not likely to seem of identical worth to different cultures in the future. As recently as twenty years ago, for example, society would not have counted uranium among its important assets.[7]

Potter thus argues that the American exploitation of resources is a basic component of the American character. We can see that the belief in the rightness of the exploitation of nature is embedded in the American belief system. Nature exists so that it may be transformed through the application of human reason, in this case, technology. Thus the abundance reaped from the soil, or from the mineral resources of the soil, becomes a truly human and therefore cultural phenomenon.

If we stop to think about this belief, we will find that it is paradoxical, in the sense that the same basic cultural premise may be used to justify radically different political and social policies. For instance, it is noteworthy that the belief that humans should control nature underlies the desires of conservationists as well as those of industrialists. These different Americans excuse their reasons for taming nature by recourse to "natural laws" and different interpretations of these laws. Conservationists argue that their control of nature would be in the best interests of "the people" but so do oil magnates. The ecologist wants to preserve bald eagles because they are "natural" (though cruel, predatory birds). Strip miners want to use the "natural" products of the earth for the good of humanity (and

5. Robert Beverly, *History and Present State of Virginia*, quoted in *The Machine in the Garden: Technology and the Pastoral Ideal in America*, ed. Leo Marx (New York: Oxford University Press, 1964), p. 85.

6. David M. Potter, *People of Plenty* (Chicago: University of Chicago Press, 1954), p. 141.

7. Ibid., p. 164.

for a profit, which, as will be discussed later, is also considered by Americans to be "natural").

Considering this constellation of beliefs as a whole, we can now add a second rewrite of the key sentence—nature plus rationality equals culture—as follows:

The laws of science and technology occupy the same position in the scheme as did the U.S. Constitution. In both cases these laws are seen to be "natural" by Americans, and their application is felt to be morally right.

It is appropriate here to point out that while in general Americans believe that the achievements of science are good, particularly when they lead to technical changes which result in "new and improved" automobiles, laundry soap, or heart transplants, there is nonetheless an ambivalence in American thinking about change. Things in nature can be seen as too artificial if somehow technology has gotten out of hand. This ambivalence is illustrated by judgments about women who use mascara, eye-shadow, lipstick, and rouge. Too lavish use of such products is regarded as producing a woman who is overly "made-up," too artificial. Yet cosmetics, particularly those which supposedly aid a woman to "look her natural best," or which render one "naturally clean," are accepted as reasonable products of human ingenuity.

This American ambivalence toward totally man-made things, seen as artificial and therefore morally suspect, is well illustrated by the American attitude toward cities, the prototype of the human-made, cultural environment. Again, the suspicion of cities evinced by Americans, like other parts of the American belief system, can be traced back to the eighteenth-century ideals. The Jeffersonian ideal included yeoman farmers, but not factory workers. This ideal was enthusiastically stated by Richard Price, an English supporter of the American Revolution:

The happiest state of man is the middle state between the *savage* and the *refined*, or between the wild and the luxurious state. Such is that state of society in CONNECTICUT, and some others of the *American* provinces; where the inhabitants consist, if I am rightly informed, of an independent and hardy YEO-MANRY, all nearly on a level—trained to arms . . . clothed in homespun—of simple manners—strangers to luxury—drawing plenty from the ground. . . the rich and the poor, the haughty grandee and the creeping sycophant, equally unknown—protected by laws, which (being their own will) cannot oppress.[8]

8. Quoted in Marx, *The Machine in the Garden*, p. 105.

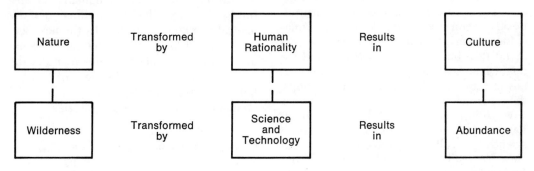

**FIGURE 1.2**
TRANSFORMATION OF THE WILDERNESS

Jefferson himself wrote that "those who labour in the earth are the chosen people of God," suggested that the United States continue to rely on Europe for manufactured goods, and commented that "the mobs of great cities add just so much to the support of pure government, as sores do to the strength of the human body."[9]

The coming of the machine was generally enthusiastically embraced by nineteenth-century Americans who saw it as a means of achieving progress and abundance for all. Yet even as most Americans were caught up with excitement over the steam engine and the railroad, there were some who saw the railroad engine as an iron monster, obscuring the purity of the land with its belching smoke. Americans continue to express ambivalence toward the machine and its works. They long to "get back to nature" but are reluctant to part with power-driven conveniences. As Leo Marx writes about twentieth-century American novelists:

Again and and again they invoke the image of a green landscape—a terrain either wild or, if cultivated, rural—as a symbolic repository of meaning and value. But at the same time they acknowledge the power of a counterforce, a machine or some other symbol of the forces which have stripped the old ideal of most, if not all, of its meaning.[10]

The American label for city political organizations reflects this ideology. City political organizations are known as "machines," considered to be "dirtier" and less moral than other kinds of politics (and we might note that "machine politics" are usually associated with urban ethnic groups, the more newly arrived immigrants). Cities have been painted as sinful and decadent, lonely and dangerous, by American social scientists as well as by people who say about New York: "It's a fine place to visit, but I wouldn't want to live there." Farm life is still seen to be more worthwhile than city life: an ambivalence toward totally man-made environments persists and sometimes leads to negative judgments about the kinds of people who live in cities as well as about cities themselves.

Several topics, including equality, individualism, and abundance have been touched on in this section. These have some basis in reality as well as in belief, which can be seen if we consider the two following points. First, the land that was to become the United States of America was relatively sparsely populated when the first European settlers arrived. It was rich in natural resources of all kinds, exploited to the point where Americans enjoy the highest standard of living in the world. Second, the American form of government was born as a result of a self-conscious attempt to create a better and more moral order—an experiment in democracy. The statement, "all men are created equal," signaled a new belief in the equality and rationality of human beings.

But as we have seen, there is a belief system underlying these facts; one that has an important role in defining "American." Americans believe that culture is created through the application of human rationality to nature. They also believe that culture invented in this way is in itself both natural and moral, unless, for other reasons, the result is judged artificial. In reverse, Americans believe that untamed nature and lawless society are less than human and cultural, and are therefore either morally neutral or morally suspect. In the next section, we will look both at the belief system underlying the American Dream and at the ways in which the development of this belief was influenced by factors of material abundance and of democratic ideals.

9. Thomas Jefferson, *Notes on Virgina,* quoted in Marx, *The Machine in the Garden:*, pp. 124-25.
10. Marx, *The Machine in the Garden:*, pp. 362-63.

## THE AMERICAN DREAM

At the time of the American Revolution, the coastal strip of land which became the United States of America had a population made up of white immigrants from northern Europe, those of British descent predominating. There were also some American Indians, and slaves and freed slaves forcibly brought over from West Africa. In the following century and a half (until laws restricting immigration were instituted in 1924), many thousands of people from most places on the globe were drawn to America. They were lured by the prospect of freedom, of riches, and of a new start in a growing country. Some of them had read or heard of the glowing promise of the Declaration of Independence that "all men are created equal" and believed that in the newly established democracy they could escape traditional overlords and create a tradition-free life. The flood of immigrants chose America as their new home because they believed in the American Dream.

In this section, we will look at some of the elements of that dream in its ideal and idealized form. The ideals presented here will be treated as if they were true, as if in fact the promises of the dream were always kept. In later chapters we will examine some of the ways in which the dream has been transformed in reality.

## FREEDOM AND WEALTH

The American dream had a foundation in the potential richness of the country. It was not simply the fertile farm lands that accounted for the allure of America. In the nineteenth century, as America became more and more highly industrialized, many immigrants came to work in city factories. Both pioneer farmers and urban laborers lived a hard life, but they were sustained by their belief that their children would do better. Their children would go to school

to learn the English language and the "American way." Then they would be able to be accepted as "real Americans" and thus to advance up the employment ladder. Hope and faith in a better future was a keystone of the dream. Optimistic faith was enough to give the immigrants strength to cut ties with relatives, friends, and familiar places, and to try their luck in the New World.

Emphasis on a shining future meant that change was not only to be expected but to be desired. Change implied progress, interpreted both in a material and a moral sense. Change in technology—the coming of mechanized factories—meant that more people could be employed, more goods turned out and sold. People would have wages to buy these goods, and their standard of living would improve. Further, technological changes were clearly seen as triumphs over raw nature through human ingenuity. Thus American scientific efforts, until very recent years, were directed toward practical ends rather than toward intellectual endeavor. The space race, for instance, represented an engineering triumph rather than a basic research coup. And if the space race produced spin-offs—cheaper nutritious breakfast drinks, for one—so much the better. Mastery over nature, whether farmland or outer space, was supposed to produce tangible benefits, to contribute materially to the general welfare.

However, "progress" is an idea that also applies to the individual American's change in social status. The ideal is upward mobility, a better job, more money, more material possessions to mark one's higher status. Upward mobility was believed to be accomplished through an individual's hard work, through the application of human rationality to living. Thus individual success is seen as morally right. As Emerson wrote:

Wealth has its source in *applications of the mind to nature,* from the rudest strokes of spade and axe up to the last secrets of art. Intimate ties subsist between thought and all production: because a better order is equivalent to vast amounts of brute labor. The forces and the resistances are nature's, but the mind acts in bringing things from where they abound to where they are wanted . . . wealth is in applications of mind to nature: and the art of getting rich consists not in industry, much less in savings, but *in a better order,* in timeliness, in being at the right spot (emphasis mine).[11]

Emerson specifically equated "applications of the mind to nature" with the acquisition of wealth and argued that wealth results in "a better order." Simple brute force, he continued, though necessary, is not sufficient but must be combined with rationality (and also, he admitted, with a little bit of luck, with "being at the right spot"). Clearly, there is a moral judgment made here that is an important part of the American Dream. Individual success, because it is the result of the individual's rational work, is morally good. In American culture one not only has the right to be upwardly mobile, one has also a moral duty to do well.

Further, Americans believe that there is an inherently right and moral mechanism which will ensure that each person is fairly rewarded for work. This mechanism is related to the notion of a free market, the idea being that the law of supply and demand will automatically guarantee that goods are sold at fair prices and that people are paid for their labor in amounts commensurate with their contribution. So if college professors earn less than plumbers, it is because college professors are not contributing directly to the general well-being of society; they are not producers of material benefits, plumbers are. Differences in pay scales, then, are also accepted by Americans as being part of the "natural order" regulated by "natural laws." Americans do *not* expect that all persons should earn an equal income; in fact, they vehemently re-

ject such ideas as "communistic." As Potter explains:

[The American] has traditionally expected to find a gamut ranging from rags to riches, from tramps to millionaires. . . . To call this "equality" may seem a contradiction in terms, but the paradox has been resolved in two ways: first, by declaring that all men are equal in the eyes of the law . . . and second, by assuming that no one is restricted or confined by his status to any one station, or even to any maximum station. Thus equality did not mean uniform position on a common level, but it did mean universal opportunity to move through a scale which transversed many levels.[12]

The belief is that "every boy *can* grow up to be president," not that every boy *will.* Those few who actually occupy the office of the president of the United States are felt to deserve such a position, particularly if they can show that through work and intelligence, they have successfully climbed the ladder from log cabin to White House. The further one travels upward from one's starting point, the more one has demonstrated virtuous success. The log cabin image is important to Americans; it symbolizes the promise of equal opportunity open to the gifted and dedicated individual.

On this ideal level, then, Americans accept differences in wealth and social status among individuals because in some sense the rich are believed to deserve their just rewards. In turn, poor and unsuccessful people are considered to be so through a lack of hard work, planning for the future, and rational thought. In American thinking there is a moral stigma attached to being poor.

11. Ralph Waldo Emerson, "Wealth," in *The American Gospel of Success,* ed. Moses Rischin (Chicago: Quadrangle Books, 1965), pp. 39-40.
12. David M. Potter, *People of Plenty* (Chicago: University of Chicago Press, 1954), p. 91.

Though most Americans acknowledge that in rich America the poor should be fed and housed, there lurks a suspicion that "those welfare chiselers" choose not to work and live high off the hog, enjoying color television at the expense of the hard-working taxpayer. This strain of American belief is sometimes called the "Protestant ethic." Its roots go back to the early European settlers, who linked work and the acquisition of property to godliness. As Cotton Mather, a famous preacher, wrote:

Every Christian ordinarily should have a *Calling*. That is to say, there should be some *Special Business*, and some *Settled Business*, wherein a Christian should for the most part spend the most of his Time: and this, so he may Glorify God, by doing *Good* for *others*, and getting of *Good* for *himself*. . . . And as a man *Impious* towards God, if he be without a *Calling*, so is he *Unrighteous* towards his *Family*, towards his *Neighborhood*, toward the *Commonwealth*, if he follow no *Calling* among them.[13]

Doing well for oneself, Mather says, is to glorify God; conversely, a man who does not work insults God, family, neighborhood, and nation. "The devil has work for idle hands" was a sentiment taken literally by early American Protestants.

We can now add two more sentences to the scheme presented in chapter 1: taken as a totality, these sentences represent the underlying beliefs of the American Dream.

Each one of these statements is connected to the others by the premise that human rationality—as expressed in social and scientific law attained through the intelligent application of human brain power to natural and social problems—produces a natural and moral result: American culture.

In looking at this diagram there are two important points to keep in mind. First, the statements in the diagram represent *beliefs* that Americans understand and share. The statements do not apply to what really happens in day-to-day social living, nor do they imply that Americans *behave* in any specific way. Nor does the diagram take into account variations of the themes expressed, nor ways in which these themes have been expanded or translated by certain American populations or at particular historic moments. In chapter 3 we will look at variation in American belief and behavior, but for the time being, we are concerned only with abstractions—ideals—which can be seen to comprise basic American culture.

Second, this set of statements must be understood in the specific American context; that is, all the statements are related to each other and also to important facts about Americans. Three of these facts have been mentioned in this chapter and can be briefly restated here: (1) all Americans are immigrants and most are fairly recent arrivals in the New World (with the exception of American Indians). American culture, then, is relatively new and is formed out of diverse elements; (2) the land that became the United States was rich in natural resources exploited to the point that Americans enjoy the highest standard of living in the world; and (3) the American government represents a self-conscious attempt to create rationally a new and better moral and social order.

These facts help give a special meaning to concepts like "abundance" or "wilderness" for Americans. While a western European might also endorse the idea expressed in sentence 2, Figure 1.3 (that nature should be tamed for human use through technology), a European would not attach the same emotional and moral value to this idea that an American would. America is a rich country; Americans live well. Americans also endorse the belief that each individual

13. Cotton Mather, "A Christian at his Calling," in *The American Gospel of Success*, ed. Moses Rischin (Chicago: Quadrangle Books, 1965), p. 24.

# AMERICAN CULTURE: AN ANTHROPOLOGICAL PERSPECTIVE
*Nature, Rationality, and the American Dream*

should have an equal opportunity under the law to achieve material success. Therefore Americans make the kinds of moral judgments they do make—about rich people and poor people, about the worth of democracy, about the desirability of change—because they believe that the individual has a chance to get a fair share of the abundance provided by nature and transformed by technology. This belief, embodied as the American Dream, involves the core set of ideal prefises listed in Figure 1.3.

The moral component of these premises leads us to a brief discussion of one more key American idea, the "melting pot." We

have traced some eighteenth-century influences on American cultural beliefs and have noticed that the most influential ideals and standards were those of the earliest European settlers, most of whom were of British origin. They and their descendents drew up the articles of government and ruled the country in its early days. The Puritan ethic was, and to a large extent still is, the Anglo-American, truly American ideal. Yet the immigrants who poured into the United States during the nineteenth and twentieth centuries were not, by and large, from England. Their language and customs were different from those of the "old settlers"; they

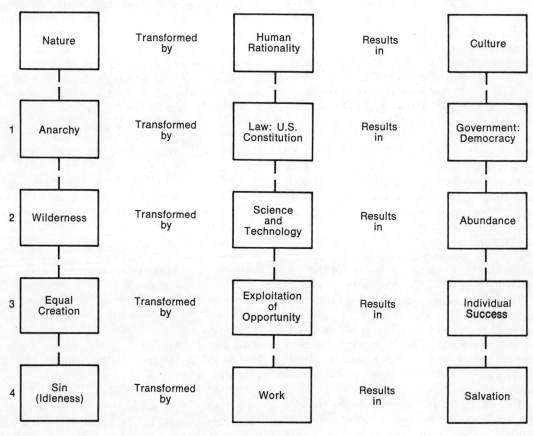

**FIGURE 1.3**
THE AMERICAN DREAM

12

had not grown up knowing the American way.

The melting pot image was evoked to try to get around the problem that these obviously non-American populations presented. It was felt that the American ideals were so compelling, so right, that in time all of these newer immigrants would be assimilated. The superior moral value of American culture would prevail, it was said. In the great melting pot of American society, differences—foreign languages and customs—would disappear; ethnic ties would be severed; and everyone would be just plain "American."

The melting pot hypothesis assumes, then, that one can learn to be an American, or that one's children can. Anthropologists assume that all people, wherever they may live, learn their culture as they grow up. So let us turn next to an examination of American beliefs about how children learn to be Americans, what kinds of things they should and do learn. In the next chapter about home, school, and work in America, we will add new sentences to the basic core of beliefs explained in this chapter.

### For Further Reading

Boorstin, Daniel J., ed. *An American Primer.* Chicago: University of Chicago Press, 1966. A useful collection of American historical documents, including commentaries written by various historians. The collection begins with the Mayflower Compact and ends with Lyndon B. Johnson's speech on voting rights.

De Tocqueville, Alexis. *Democracy in America.* Translated by Henry Reeve. New York: Vintage Books, 1961 (orig. 1835). Perhaps the most famous and still one of the most perceptive analyses of the American experiment in democracy, written by a young French aristocrat in the early nineteenth century.

Potter, David. *People of Plenty.* Chicago: University of Chicago Press, 1954. A historian's viewpoint on the relative influence of the frontier and of material abundance on the American character.

Rischin, Moses, ed. *The American Gospel of Success.* Chicago: Quadrangle Books, 1965. A collection of documents which show American attitudes toward material wealth and success from colonial days to the present.

### Bibliography

Boorstin, Daniel J., ed. 1966. *An American Primer.* Chicago: University of Chicago Press.

Dumont, Louis 1970. *Homo Hierarchicus.* Chicago: University of Chicago Press.

Marx, Leo, ed. 1964. *The Machine in the Garden: Technology and the Pastoral Ideal in America.* New York: Oxford University Press.

Potter, David 1954. *People of Plenty.* Chicago: University of Chicago Press.

Rischin, Moses, ed. 1965. *The American Gospel of Success.* Chicago: Quadrangle Books.

# 2 | Home, School and Work: Learning to Be American

In this section we will look at the ways in which Americans learn that set of shared beliefs and shared understandings about the meaning of symbols previously defined as "culture." In America this learning is accomplished in two major ways. First, the child from its birth learns *informally* in its home and through interaction with friends and relatives. Second, the American child is sent to school to learn *formally* under the direction of professional teachers.

When they are young, children learn a language. They also learn rules regarding their behavior towards their parents and other relatives and regarding playing with their peers. They learn other things too—the culturally appropriate ways of eating, "good table manners," for instance—as well as what things are defined as good to eat. Americans learn that beef, particularly that part of the steer called "steak," is a preferred food, while they learn to show disgust at the idea of someone eating insects.

As children grow older, they become familiar with myths and folklore; they are taught religious beliefs and observances of holidays. They become adept in recognizing and using the technical resources of their environment, from toothbrushes to computers. They are urged to learn certain cognitive skills, reading and writing at least. Much of this learning, in America, is geared

toward the goal of success, of upward mobility, which is closely related to the kind of job and income an adult can obtain. Therefore in this chapter we will consider the relationships among three different spheres of American life: home, school, and work.

It is not surprising that anthropologists have been interested in the American family and kinship system because in social anthropology, the study of kinship and the family has occupied a central place. Anthropologists concentrate on kinship and family structure in their work in nonliterate societies because other institutions—political, economic, or religious—are most often organized along kinship lines in traditional society. However, this is not, or at least is not supposed to be, the case in American society. Americans make clear distinctions between family or kinship relationships on the one hand; economic, political, religious, and work relationships on the other. In fact in most places in America this distinction appears in laws forbidding a political figure to hire a relative, or prohibiting a husband and wife from holding jobs in the same state-supported university.

These antinepotism laws make a legal distinction between the world of work and the home world. Americans feel that the kinds of relationships and activities found in the world of work and the home world are quite different. *Private life* exists within the family, while *public life* takes place in a nonkinship setting. Within the family, Americans believe, relationships among people are, or should be, loving, close, cooperative, and enduring.[1] But outside the family, the world-of-work relationships are seen to be impersonal, competitive, and transient. Jules Henry, in his book about American culture, *Culture Against Man,* locates those motives for action he calls *drives*—competition, the drive for security and a higher standard of living—in the work world. By contrast, gentleness, kindness, and generosity exist in the home.[2] The school world, however, is neither part of the home world nor the work world. School is not kinship-based, and children go to school to "work" and to compete. But the kind of work they do is not paid and is seen to be a preparation for "real" work. And although school friends are not "family," relationships with peers at school can be close and enduring. Further, the institution of the public school in American society is unique because virtually all children growing up in America spend many hours each day for many years attending school. A great deal of the responsibility for turning children into adults and for producing "good citizens" belongs to the public school system. Thus the world of school stands between the worlds of home and work and must be considered with them as we look at the ways in which people become "American" and at what being "American" implies.

## THE AMERICAN FAMILY

As Schneider has said,

The family [the American premise is that:] stands for how kinship should be conducted and, because they are members of the family, it stands at the same time for how the husband and wife and their children conduct themselves.[3]

The assumption is made that if family behavior is "right," then nothing will go wrong in the larger society. On the other hand, high divorce rates, alcoholism, drug abuse, crime, poverty, and juvenile delinquency are often blamed on "wrong" family relationships. As a consequence, one must look closely at beliefs about the American family because the family and relationships within it are considered both to reflect the state of society and to be a cause of social well-being or of social ills.

As I stated before, Americans believe that relationships within the family should be loving, close, cooperative, and enduring. In other words, family relationships are based on emotional ties, on affect. A new family is created through marriage. The choice of a partner is personal; it involves "love." Most Americans are shocked to learn that in many societies, marriage is arranged by the older kin of the bride and groom and may be preceded by lengthy negotiations over the transfer of valuables from the prospective groom's kin to the future bride's kin. Marriage, for Americans, should be based on mutual attraction and consent; one should not marry for money or because one's parents desire an alliance with a rich or powerful family. Instead, the wishes and feelings of the individual man or woman are of primary importance.

1. David M. Schneider, *American Kinship* (Englewood Cliffs, N. J.: Prentice-Hall, 1968).

2. Jules Henry, *Culture Against Man* (New York: Vintage Books, 1965).

3. Schneider, *American Kinship*, p. 44. As mentioned, there is a substantial amount of scholarly work on the American family and on American kinship, much of it fairly technical. There is no attempt here to review such work, particularly that on kinship terminology because I am more interested in laying out the broad outlines of the American belief system.

It is also true for Americans that sex and marriage are inextricably linked. While today it is somewhat more permissible than it was thirty years ago for young men and young women to engage in sexual relations without being married, Americans still believe that a sexual relationship should involve a marriagelike emotion of love. Even if sex before marriage is not "really" immoral, it is still considered somewhat deviant. Sexual relationships within marriage, however, are so highly valued that sexual incompatibility between marriage partners may be grounds for divorce.

So the kind of love that creates a marriage and results in the birth of children and in a family is sexual love. But marriage and family are not synonymous in American culture, as the saying "they're married but they don't have a family" indicates. People also speak of having another child "to complete the family." Children conceived "out of wedlock" are "natural children" and may be referred to in law and in common speech as "illegitimate." Sexual intercourse, then, creates both a marriage and eventually a family, but for Americans sexual intercourse must be lawfully certified by a religious or civil ceremony. Americans say that human sexuality is "natural" and insist that men and women are "naturally" attracted to one another. But sexuality untamed, unregulated, is suspect. It is only through the application of law to "natural" sexual relations that humans attain fully "human" nature and create the human family. The family in American culture provides the archtypical case of the transformation of nature into culture through reason. The American family, then, consists of a man and a woman who, married to each other, have children. In social science terminolgy this type of family is called a *nuclear family* and may be diagrammed as follows:[4]

When I say that the American family is nuclear and show a diagram labeled "nu-

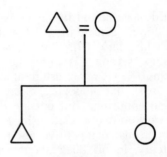

**FIGURE 2.1**
THE NUCLEAR FAMILY

clear famliy," what is the implication? Obviously, many American families do not really consist of just those people in the diagram—one mother, one father, one son, one daughter. We know too that there are many divorced couples in America and also that not all American children are conceived within a legal marriage. It is important to understand, then, that when I say that the American family is nuclear, I am making a statement about American culture, the system of shared beliefs and understandings. In other words, in this chapter, as in chapter one, we are talking about *beliefs* about American culture, about ideals and ideal types rather than about the ways in which these ideals are acted out by real people. Sometimes American beliefs are also written as laws and thus in society recognized as *norms*—rules for behavior that state the ways in which people *ought* to behave. But obviously, the statement of a rule doesn't guarantee that all people will follow it. Some people don't always stop their cars at a

4. In diagrams of this sort, triangles represent males, and circles represent females. An equal = sign indicates a marriage; a slash through an equal sign ≠ indicates that the marriage has ended in divorce. Horizontal lines connecting triangles or circles ( △ ○ △ ) show that these individuals are *siblings*, that is, brother or sister to one another. A vertical line indicates a parent-child relationship, or *descent* ( ○ ).

stop light. Some children are not always obedient to their parents. In other words, behavior often varies from the norm. And among certain American populations there exist norms which represent variations from the general cultural base we are considering here.

These three considerations—cultural beliefs, normative rules, and observed behaviors—may in any one situation contradict each other. This point can be illustrated by referring to the antinepotism laws. Antinepotism laws mark the cultural distinction between the world of work and the home world. They also embody a legal norm, expressing a belief about how people ought to act. But the political reality in many towns and cities is that relatives of a winning candidate for public office stand to gain. For instance, John F. Kennedy, when he became president, appointed his brother Robert to the cabinet post of attorney general. Yet the *rule* on both a cultural and sociolegal level remains that kinship relationships should be nonoperative in politics. Americans know and understand this rule, but they sometimes break it. For one thing, it conflicts with another cultural belief, that "blood is thicker than water." For some Americans this cultural belief overrides the home-work opposition. Americans distinguish between "blood relatives" and relatives by marriage. Blood relatives are

felt to be the "closest," and the ties with them the strongest, deepest, and most enduring. So rewarding one's brother with a political post can be seen as being loyal to one's family. Thus Americans can understand why a politician would support antinepotism rules only when they did not apply to his or her own relatives, even though they still endorse the *principle* that family ties should have no influence on political behavior.

We can now turn back to the discussion of marriage and the family, and write another sentence to add to the description of the American belief system begun in chapter 1.

The entry under "culture" again implies a moral judgment (and in this case also embodies a normative rule for behavior). We can look at two variations of the American family (again seen here as ideal types) to show how moral judgments are applied to families which are believed to vary from the nuclear model.

The single-parent family is a common occurrence in American society. Divorce, separation, or death creates a unit from which one parent, often but not always the father, is missing. Since one of the parent slots is not filled, this unit is reduced from the nuclear ideal and is often called by Americans "a broken home." This terminology implies a moral judgment which is in fact often

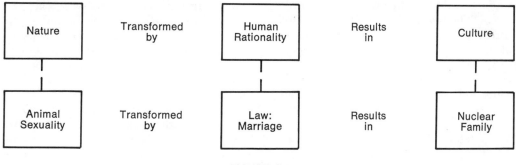

**FIGURE 2.2**
LOVE AND MARRIAGE

17

called up. Social ills like juvenile delinquency and drug-taking, and personality disorders ranging from mild neuroticism to schizophrenia are often blamed on "broken homes." Further, a high divorce rate is often believed to be an indication of the collapse of the moral fabric of society and a harbinger of doom for America in general.

Another common variation of the nuclear family is not censured so strongly but is still felt to be somewhat deviant and inconvenient. This type is what anthropologists call an *extended family*. The term refers to families containing more than the two generations—parent and child—present in the nuclear family. An extended family might consist of a man and his wife and their married son, his wife, and children. Extended families are not felt to be really immoral, but their existence violates another rule pertaining to the American family—a *residence rule of neolocality*. Americans, when they marry, are expected to move out of their parents' homes and establish a new residence for themselves. They are then expected to be independent of their parents. Financial considerations may force young couples to live with the parents of one of them, but ideally, this joint residence will be for a short time only. In fact, if a grown, married man with children continues to reside with his parents, he may be accused of not being "man enough" to support his family, or he may be supposed to be not yet adult, still "tied to his mother's apron strings." Though one's parents are blood relatives and thus very "close," the rule of neolocality, and the ideology of independent individualism and self-reliance dictate that one should at marriage sever ties to parents and establish a home of one's own. When one's parents become old or ill and unable to fend for themselves, they may again be reunited with their children, "taken in." But, on the other hand, as older people they may reside instead in nursing homes or retirement communities. The ideal is the self-sufficient and complete nuclear family whose members live together. Therefore reduced nuclear families or extended families are seen as deviant and sometimes as immoral.

The closed nature of the nuclear family is related to the idea of "blood relationships" mentioned earlier. Americans believe that children share equally in the biogenetic substance of their mothers and fathers. The child is not more "closely" related to father or to mother, nor to father's kin than to mother's kin. Both mother's sister and father's sister, for instance, are considered to be equally related to their sibling's child, who calls them by the term "aunt." The more biogenetic substance one shares with a relative, the "closer" is that relative; a "half-sister," for instance, is less close than a full sister. The closest relatives, of course, are the members of one's own nuclear family—from the child's point of view, "mother," "father," "sister," and "brother." "Closeness" defined by "blood" is related to emotional "closeness"; it is assumed that emotional ties among the members of the nuclear family will be most intense, most enduring, most loving.

But the kind of love that obtains between blood relatives is opposite to the sexual love between husband and wife. Husband and wife are not blood relatives. In fact, according to custom and to law, blood relatives, particularly "close" relatives, are prohiibted from marrying. Those relatives who are judged "too close" to be marriageable are also felt to be sexually unavailable because sex and marriage go together in American culture. The list includes one's mother and father, one's sister and brother, one's children and, for many Americans, one's first cousin. Marriage between these relatives is banned by both tradition and written law. In some states there is a longer list, including more distant relatives—like a grandfather's wife—whom one cannot marry by law; but for most Americans, the desirability of choosing a mate who is approximately the same age rules out relatives who are much younger or much older.[5] However, this general set of laws and customs does mean that relatives usually will not marry, and that husband and wife are therefore not kin to each other. So the American family contains two distinct kinds of love, one appropriate for kin and one for nonkin. One is symbolized by sexual intercourse between husband and wife, and the other by shared blood. These two unite and define the nuclear family.

### HOME AND WORK: FEMALE AND MALE

Relationships based on closeness and permanence and involving solace and tenderness—that is, love relationships—serve to differentiate the world of home and family from the world of work. In the outside world of public affairs Americans do not expect to find loving relationships. It is clear that the personality traits Turner attributed to the influence of the frontier—coarseness and strength; acuteness and inquisitiveness; restlessness and nervous energy; and dominant individualism—have their place in the work world but not in the home. They do not fit in with the ideal picture of the American family relationships we have been describing.

Turner believed these qualities to be "uniquely American," yet if we look more closely at them we can see that qualities such as strength and coarseness are those Americans associate with men rather than with women. On the other hand, the qualities of gentleness, cooperation, and love are felt by Americans to be associated more with women than with men. Let us look at these male-female distinctions together with the home-work distinction with a view to understanding why love is the symbol that stands for the home and family, while other qualities are brought into play in the world of work.

The American family by definition includes children. Americans consider that it is natural for a married couple to want children. However, Americans also believe that women, rather than men, "naturally" like children and can better care for them. The prime job of a woman is to care for her children and her house; Americans say "a woman's place is in the home." Therefore because a family is the place where children are raised, and women are "naturally" child-producers and child-caretakers, the "inside" world of home and family is coded "female," while the "outside" world of work is coded "male."

The "inside" world is female in two senses. First, at home within the bounds of the nuclear family, a man may relax, he may and should show love and emotion that would be "unmanly" to exhibit at work. American men at work are expected to be "tough." American men unlike French or Italian men, for instance, do not embrace or kiss each other on the street when they meet; they shake hands instead. American women, however, may kiss each other in greeting; they may also cry in public. They are believed to be "naturally" more sweet and loving, more emotional and expressive than men. Thus for the American man, signs of strong emotion in public, at work, might be counted as signs of effeminancy. Only within his home is he permitted a certain amount of "feminine," i.e., emotional, behavior.

Second, the inside world is coded "female" because women in American culture dominate that world. Men go "out" to work, leaving the responsibility of the house and children to their wives. This burden defines an American woman as socially adult. Through marriage and child-bearing she

5. See Karl G. Heidler, "Anthropological Models of Incest Laws in the United States," *American Anthropologist* 71 (1969), pp. 693-701, for a more complete treatment of variations in laws forbidding incest.

earns the title "Mrs." and assumes a status within society determined by her husband's status. It is often taken for granted that a young wife will continue an "outside" job for a time, but it is understood that her prime social identity and personal fulfillment will come through her husband and children, through her activities at home within the family.

On the other hand, while marriage and children are taken as a sign that a young man has "settled down" and is therefore more mature and responsible, yet the identity of an American male is more tied to his successful performance of a good "outside" job than it is to his successful performance of his role as husband and father. In fact his ability to fulfill the expectations set up by the husband-father roles may be determined by his job opportunities and success. As Liebow has pointed out in his discussion of black street-corner men, the fact that these men find it hard to get and hold decent, well-paying jobs means that they find it difficult to support a wife and children. They count marriage as a sign of manliness and maturity, but they are often forced to separate from their wives and children for economic reasons. The job pays too little, the wife complains, and the husband, feeling resentful and unsuccessful, moves out. Because they are deprived of a satisfactory chance to prove themselves to be socially acceptable adult males in the culturally approved way, they are denied permanent home and family ties.

For an American male, then, his position in the "outside" world often affects his chances for a successful family life. For American women, on the other hand, "womanliness" or "femininity" are not determined by job performance on the "outside" (although 40 percent of American women do work outside the home), but rather on marital status and relationships to children. Similarly, though American men certainly father children, they are often excluded

from intimate relationships with them. They are away from home in the daylight hours and interact with children only at breakfast and at bedtime. Fathers may become strangers in their own homes, viewed by both their wives and children as interlopers. The male-female line separating "inside" from "outside" is hard for either men or women to cross.[6]

## LEARNING AT HOME

By being a part of an American family, what kinds of things does a child learn about being "American"? As we have seen, he or she is exposed to sex-role differentiation. Parents teach the accepted sex-typical behavior to children both consciously and unconsciously. "Nice little girls don't fight," a mother might say to her daughter; but in a similar situation she might ask her son, "Why didn't you hit him back?" Girls are prepared for the feminine world of home and family, while boys learn rougher behavior more appropriate to the world of work. They both become aware of the "inside-outside" distinction. They know that Daddy goes "out to work," even though as young children they may have a very hazy idea of what Daddy does when he is away from home.

Obviously, children learn to talk, and in most cases they learn American English. They learn kinship terms, and they learn that "mother" is "closer" than "aunt." They are usually told, "No, you can't marry Mommy (or Daddy) when you grow up," though the reasons given for this prohibition may be vague. They learn that family relationships are, or should be, loving and enduring, and that the kind of love expressed by father and mother for each other is dif-

6. Lucy Garretson-Selby, *The Nature of American Women: A Cultural Account* (Austin: University of Texas, 1972).

ferent in kind from that shown by Mommy or Daddy for their children.

Much of this knowledge is not explicitly taught, but American parents are often very explicit and very concerned with other kinds of learning and development in children. Americans feel that children develop more fully each year. Each new accomplishment —weaning, toilet training, walking, learning the letters of the alphabet—is thought of as a step upward The child is not only growing physically bigger but better and smarter as well. The child's accomplishment is seen also as an accomplishment of the parents, particularly of the child's mother. For while bearing and rearing children are considered "natural" by Americans, they are also considered difficult. Experts are consulted, special doctors to advise one on the child's health and diet, other doctors to tell one how to handle temper tantrums or sibling rivalry. The American mother must keep up with the latest scientific knowledge about child-raising which, like other American activities, is judged successful and good when the "naturalness" of the activity is tempered with rationality, represented by science, technology, or medicine. American mothers rely on experts to tell them what to feed their children, what the child should play with or wear, what kind of crib should be bought. Technological complexity and material abundance have created throwaway baby bottles as well as space rockets.

The emphasis on progress and the belief in continuing abundance make it possible for American mothers to embrace new methods and new material aids in child-raising. One thing American children learn, then, is that new things are best and that old or broken things should be discarded. Children are also taught that personal cleanliness is highly desirable; for instance, that feces are dirty and should be disposed of by means of the flush toilet as soon as possible. The child sees too that the household trash is taken outside and disappears. Chil-

dren are admonished to wash their hands before eating, to keep out of the mud, to brush their teeth. The maxim is that "cleanliness is next to godliness." Thus children learn that what is new and clean is better than what is old and dirty. They learn, like their mothers and fathers, to want new things. In a word, they learn to be consumers.

Again, the notion of progress, coupled with the notion of the inexhaustibility of the rich resources of the land and its people, logically leads to expectations of high consumption of new things. If you view the world as a bottomless treasure box in which the most valuable and worthwhile goods are stashed at deeper and deeper levels of the box, then you are willing to trade in what you have at the present for an expected improvement. Technological innovations in communication, particularly television, make it possible for every American, including American children, to know about the latest toothpaste or the newest toy. The importance of advertising in American life has prompted one anthropologist, Jules Henry, to consider that the fundamental orientation of Americans is:

. . . towards private property, the high rising standard of living, competition, achievement and security. Thus the *stupified* TV audience is the natural and necessary complement to the *alert* adverstiser; and the merchants of *confusion* on Madison Avenue are a necessary complement to hard-pressed industry, pursuing economically *rational* ends . . . [The American] desire for a higher living standard makes them susceptible to the advertising that assails them with increasing pressure to raise it (italics original).[7]

Henry feels that the American consumer's habits represent a perversion of the Amer-

7. Henry, *Culture Against Man* (New York: Vintage Books, 1965), p. 96.

ican Dream of abundance for all. While we do not have to agree completely with his point of view, we can acknowledge that advertising does reach American children—through television, newspapers, and even cereal boxes—and that, like their parents, American children learn to want new and presumably better material goods. By the time the American child goes to school, he or she is familiar with many of the consumer goods produced by American technology. Television and TV dinners, automobiles and toy electric cars, plastic food wrap, and clothes made of synthetic materials are all part of daily life. They are to be taken for granted, along with electricity, indoor plumbing, and heat. Television brings knowledge of these staples of American life to almost all American children, even those whose parents barely make enough money to put food on the table. Thus a knowledge of the nature of the material world and assumptions about the desirability of obtaining goods become a part of shared American culture.

Before we go on to consider the world of school, we can sum up some of the basic things the American child has learned about American culture. First, he or she has learned to distinguish between male and female, between the world of home and the world of work. The child has learned to distinguish different kinds of relatives and the rules of behavior toward them. The child has learned that old, worn-out things are trash and should be thrown away, that new things are better than old. The child has also begun to understand that life is like a ladder, that each valued new achievement places one on a higher rung.

The ladder image becomes important early to the child, who soon learns that certain kinds of behavoir are said to be "babyish" and that "big girls and boys" act differently. Words like "baby," "toddler," and "preschooler" mark different age-grades for American children before they ever get to school. American children learn that the older one is, the higher one's age-grade, the more responsibilities and privileges one obtains. A "responsible teenager" is allowed to use the car, while a "preadolescent" is not. Clothing for children, particularly for girls, is also age-graded according to criteria of height and body shape. Department stores have different sections, starting with "babies" and "toddlers" (which sell clothes for both boys and girls) and continuing, for females, through "girls," "subteens," "preteens," "teens," and "juniors" to "women's." Obviously, as children grow they need bigger sizes of clothing, but the point is that in America these different sizes and shapes of clothing have official commercial names that mark age-grade status as well as physical growth.

These age-grade distinctions shade into one another; there is no exact moment at which a child becomes a "boy" or "girl" instead of a "toddler." Nor in America are there any ceremonies that mark a child's physical maturity, usually attained when the American child is in his or her early teens and not yet considered an adult. Nor is there a ceremony to mark a person's becoming "adult." Yet the one firm distinction and opposition is between "adult" and all other age-grades. Adults are responsible working people who have the power in society; nonadults are seen as essentially nonserious people who do not work or take care of families and who traditionally are barred from the exercise of power. While preschool children may not have learned the subtle distinction between "preteens" and "teens" by the time they reach first grade, they know that there is a basic difference between the "grown-ups" and the "kids."

By this time most children have also begun to understand another important social distinction: the difference between people who are "like us" and those who are "not like us." This distinction may be made on economic, racial, religious, neighborhood, or kinship lines, and is inevitable simply because the American population is not homogeneous. Distinctions between people "like us" and other people are reinforced by the application of an unwritten rule applying to American marriage. This rule is that marriage should be *homogamous*, which means that, ideally, husband and wife should be more or less equally matched in age, education, economic background, ethnic background, race, religion, and so forth. With the exception of the now-defunct laws prohibiting interracial marriage, the homogamy principles are not encoded in civil law but are well understood by Americans nevertheless. The marriage of a Catholic to a Jew, or of an older woman to a younger man, for instance, are believed to be "difficult" and liable to end in divorce. In fact, most Americans do marry someone "like" themselves and teach their children to know how they are different from "other people."

## LEARNING IN SCHOOL: THE LADDER ASSUMPTION

In school the process of learning to be American continues, though some cultural themes are stressed and others ignored. For instance, although children may like and respect some teachers, they are not expected to love them in the same way they love their parents. Home values of enduring solidarity and cooperation between loving people are not foremost in school. On the contrary, children must learn to adjust to new authority, new places like "the principal's office," new concepts of time, and new rules for behavior. School is a place where children learn to stand in line, to fold their hands and listen quietly to the teacher, to write their names neatly at the top right-hand corner of their papers. Docile behavior is appropriate in the classroom, but more active behavior is all right at recess. Children learn that what they must know is divided into "subjects," taught at certain regular times called "periods" or "classes." They learn that if they are "good" and "intelligent," they will be rewarded with "good grades" and will be "promoted."

Generally speaking, I am not concerned here with the subject matter—reading or algebra—that American children are supposed to master in school, except for those portions of the school curriculum—American history, for example—which relate directly to learning to be American. Instead, I want to look at the ways in which cultural assumptions are introduced or reinforced in American public schools. Let us consider the meaning of some of the words in the preceding paragraph: "good grades," "intelligence," "promotion."

American parents believe that each achievement of their young child is a sign of progress and success. This idea is very strongly encoded in the public schools. Children start out in first grade and every year are supposed to progress higher, to master more and more difficult tasks, until finally they complete twelfth grade and "graduate." They may then go on to an institution of "higher" learning. The more grades one completes, the higher the prestige one has, and the more one is presumed to have succeeded. To be a dropout is to admit to failure; it implies either that one has not worked hard enough, or that one is not intelligent.

Remember that Americans place a high moral value on work and on human rationality. While all men are created equal, that is, with rational faculties, not all are equally rational or equally hardworking in developing their rational potential. Thus laziness and stupidity, while not exactly the same thing, are closely linked in the American mind. A person who doesn't do well in school, then, is suspected of being "stubborn," of "not trying," or of having a low intelligence quotient (IQ). Americans have developed various tests which they believe scientifically measure a child's IQ, and they

23

believe that it is "natural" that some children should have higher IQs than others. But they also believe that "natural" problems or difficulties can be solved through human ingenuity, and they therefore create special classes for children with low IQs, the idea being that special teaching will enable these children to "catch up" or at least "hold their own." If they don't, Americans reason, it must be that they aren't working hard enough.

So American children in school learn that there is a ladderlike progression of grades and also that there are "grades" within "grades," that is, that there are differences among children of the same age. Some of these differences are coded by letters, A, B, C, D, and F. Children quickly learn than an A is better than a C. Children also quickly understand the system when schools "stream" their students, putting the "quicker" ones in one classroom and the "slow learners" in another. Miss Brown's students *know* that they are supposed to be brighter than Mrs. Green's, and Mrs. Green's students *know* they are supposed to be "the dumb kids." The institution of the American public school, then, does not create out of whole cloth the idea that progress, achievement, and hard work are desirable, but it strongly reinforces this American tenant.

Competition, grading, and the achievement ladder in American schools are felt by Americans to be important because schooling—education—is seen as the pathway to upward mobility, to individual success. American parents feel that their children should do well in school and should stay in school for as many years as possible because it will increase their chances for good jobs. There is some recent data that support this belief. Jencks has found, using the Duncan scale which assigns ratings from zero to ninety-six to various occupations (ninety-six being the most prestigious and well-paid occupation), that each extra year of schooling equals six points on this scale. In other words, a high-school graduate is likely to have a job that rates twelve points higher than the job a person who completed tenth grade would be likely to have. Jencks also found that there was a high correlation between a man's educational attainment and his occupational status.[8] So the American interest and anxiety over educational attainment has some real meaning in the world of work.

Another reason for the stress on education in America is that schools are believed to teach one how to be a "good American." Schools are seen as socializing agents, which will teach children the values of democracy and the meaning of the free enterprise system and will acquaint them with traditional American beliefs and myths. The socializing function of the school became of prime importance when so many new immigrants arrived in America in the nineteenth century. Many of these immigrants did not even speak English; their arrival sparked the spread of the public school system and in some measure changed the way in which educators saw schools. Schools became not simply a place where one learned certain cognitive skills. The meaning of education expanded to include "civilizing immigrants,"[9] teaching them to speak English and to salute the flag, to understand simple arithmetic, and to know that George Washington "could not tell a lie." Classes in cooking and sewing, woodworking and metal shop were also introduced into the schools to show the immigrants the "American way." The schools were seen as an important aid in homogenizing the population, in helping the melting pot to work.

8. Christopher Jencks, *Inequality* (New York: Harper & Row, 1972), p. 181.
9. Bud B. Kheif, "The School as a Small Society," in *To See Ourselves: Anthropology and Modern Social Issues,* ed. Thomas Weaver (Glenview, Ill.: Scott, Foresman and Co., 1973), p. 282.

Margaret Mead has pointed out that the second-generation immigrants learned to be ashamed of their parents' foreign ways, tried hard to be 100 percent English-speaking, hamburger-eating Americans, working their way upward out of the urban slums. Third-generation Americans, Mead argues, expect to be different from their parents only in the sense that they feel they ought to achieve ever higher levels of success. Metaphorically speaking, Mead says, virtually all Americans are "third generation." Since very few Americans are descendants of the Founding Fathers, the historical myth taught in school assumes a symbolic role:

[The European observer] hears an endless invocation of Washington and Lincoln, of Jefferson and Franklin. Obviously, Americans go in for ancestor worship, says the European. Obviously, Americans are longing for a strong father, say the psychoanalysts. These observers miss the point that Washington is not the ancestor of the man who is doing the talking: Washington does not represent the past to which one belongs by birth, but the past to which one tries to belong by effort. . . . This odd blending of the future and the past, in which another man's great-grandfather becomes the symbol of one's grandson's future, is an essential part of American culture.[10]

Beliefs about the rightness and morality of the American government are reinforced by presenting the Founding Fathers as idealized figures. It wasn't that George Washington *did* not tell lie—he *could* not. For American school children he is presented as a superhuman, a mythic figure, a symbol of the American belief that their country and its form of government is morally right. American children, as Mead points out, realize their uneasy "third-generation" status in school, through competition to "do better," while at the same time learning that being a patriotic Ameri-

can requires adherence to a belief in the rightness of historic myths.

I have mentioned that American children learn in school that there are differences among them based on grades of two kinds and on "intelligence." School also reinforces the learning, begun at home, that there are "people like me" and "people different from me," based partly on the criterion of performance in school and partly on ethnic, racial, religious, sexual, economic, or even geographic distinctions. For instance, Southern children learn about "damyankees." Within a single school, children meet those of whom their parents have said, "they're not like us"; and children tend to spend more time with those they judge are "like us." Hollingshead's book, *Elmtown's Youth,* shows that friendship groups within a school are made up of children whose parents have more or less equal status outside the school and, further, that children of high-status parents enjoy high status within the school too. Inequalities or differences within the school reflect home and work differences among people outside the school. So while schools are believed to achieve melting-pot goals, to mold children from different backgrounds into homogeneous "good Americans," children also learn in school that there are different kinds of Americans and that some of them, the richer or smarter perhaps have a higher status. Children learn that "all men are created equal" in nature, but that there are "natural" differences among them in human culture.

### CONCLUSION

In this chapter, we have looked at the American family in some detail from a cultural point of view. I have said that children learn role differentiation based on sex;

10. Margaret Mead, *And Keep Your Powder Dry* (New York: William Morrow and Company, 1965, orig. 1942), pp. 49-50.

they learn basic distinctions between the world of home and the world of work, and they begin to understand American beliefs about success and upward mobility. In school the hierarchical progression of grades and the grading within each grade reinforce ideas about the nature of success in American culture. Children also acquire knowledge of cultural patriotic beliefs in school: they learn about concepts like "democracy," and "free enterprise," and the "American way." They learn to believe that a successful and long school career will prepare them better for success in the world of work, which they believe will be competitive and graded much like school, except that material possessions instead of As will be the mark of success.

So far the American cultural system has been described in general terms. I have discussed basic shared American beliefs, rather than the specific beliefs and actions of one particular group of Americans. In the next chapter, we will turn from this general discussion to a review of studies that have been undertaken with a view to understanding what real groups of Americans, in real towns, on street corners, in bars, are like. As I have said, children learn early that not all Americans are the same. We will look at specific groups of Americans in chapter 3, while in chapter 4, we will attempt to understand variety in American culture.

### For Further Reading

Mead, Margaret. *And Keep Your Powder Dry*. New York: William Morrow and Company, 1965 (orig. 1942). Although the sections of this book which were intended to show how to boost morale during World War II are somewhat dated, Mead's general outline of the American character remains interesting.

Romney, A. Kimball and Roy G. D'Andrade. "Cognitive Aspects of English Kin Terms," *American Anthropologist* 66 (1964), pp. 146-170. An analysis of kin terms and their meanings for Americans.

Schneider, David M. *American Kinship*. Englewood Cliffs, N. J.: Prentice-Hall, 1968. The most thorough attempt to construct a cultural model of American kinship and the family. Schneider also takes into account variations in kin term usage and describes the ways in which people may count others as relatives.

Slater, Philip. *The Pursuit of Loneliness: American Culture at the Breaking Point*. Boston: Beacon Press, 1970. As the title indicates, this is a pessimistic assessment of American culture and American character.

### Bibliography

Henry, Jules. 1965. *Culture Against Man*. New York: Vintage Books.

Schneider, David M. 1968. *American Kinship: A Cultural Account*. Englewood Cliffs, N. J.: Prentice-Hall.

# 3 | Variations on American Themes

The first two chapters of this book were concerned with presenting a sketch of the American belief system and its moral entailments. So far, we have avoided questions about variations within the culture and have concentrated instead on broad cultural outlines. In this chapter we will look at some of the studies of specific American communities, institutions, and groups in order to document the extent to which the American Dream and the American reality are in agreement. How are ideas like "equality," "democracy," or "the nuclear family" translated into everyday life? To what extent do these ideas mean the same thing for different groups of Americans? Questions like these will be the focus of this chapter.

## THE DISCOVERY OF SOCIAL CLASS

According to the postulates of the American Dream, all men are created equal. Social differences between them will result only because different individuals will work harder and thus, deservedly, be more successful; they will have more money. This was the assumption held by W. Lloyd Warner in the 1930s as he began his research on "Yankee City" (Newburyport, Massachusetts). Warner had previously done fieldwork among the Australian ab-

origines and was familiar with the intricacies of Australian kinship systems. But he thought that in an American town he would find a relatively simple social system in which differences among people or groups of people could be directly related to differences in economic status. As he puts it, he originally believed that:

The most vital and far-reaching value systems which motivate Americans are to be ultimately traced to an economic order.[1]

However, as Warner and his associates began to talk to the people of Yankee City and to observe their actions, they discovered to their surprise that, while economic factors were important in determining a person's social status, they could not explain all social differences between people or groups of people. Economic factors alone did not explain why all doctors, for instance, were not ranked equally by Yankee City people. Nor could economic factors totally explain the existence of social boundaries between groups of people. Social reality in Yankee City did not conform to the ideal of equality tempered only by individual

1. Lloyd Warner, ed., *Yankee City*, rev. ed. in 1 vol. (New Haven, Conn.: Yale University Press, 1963), p. 35.

achievement; instead, it was clear that in Yankee City, at least, some men were created more equal than others. Further, there were social boundaries that divided groups of people into more or less stable units which Warner decided to call "social classes."

He found that while occupation and wealth did matter—that is, a millworker would not be considered "upper class"—upward mobility was constrained to a large degree by intangible factors like "manners," "knowing how to behave," belonging to the "right" church and the "right" civic organizations. Further, people were judged to "know how to behave," and they were admitted to the "right" clubs only if they had the "right" language, religion, and skin color. In short, language, religion, and race to a great degree determined social status.

Warner found that skin color, or "race," was an absolute marker of social differences. He listed five racial types in order of their social ranking: (1) light caucasoids, (2) dark caucasoids, (3) mongoloids and caucasoid mixtures that look caucasoid, (4) mongoloid and caucasoid mixtures that look mongoloid, and (5) Negroes and all negroid mixtures. In regard to religion and language, English speakers outranked all others, while Protestantants ranked higher than Catholics, who ranked higher than nonChristians. In other words, Warner found that white Anglo-Saxon Protestants (WASPs) were most likely to be found on the top of the social heap.

The very most prestigious class in Yankee City, called by Warner the "upper-upper class," consisted of "old family"—descendants of early settlers in the town whose fortunes had been made in past decades and who now lived in eighteenth-century houses on top of the hill. The next class was the "lower-upper"—people who had money but who were not old family—followed by the "upper-middle class," professional people. The "lower-middle" and "upper-lower"

classes were comprised of small businessmen and millworkers and laborers, respectively. The "lower-lower class" was made up of people who were out of work, were criminals, or were judged deviant in some other way.

The existence of this six-class system came as a surprise to Warner and his associates. They were also surprised to discover that social mobility between classes was much more limited than Americans had believed. For instance, it was almost impossible in Yankee City for a person to belong to the upper-upper class unless he or she had been born into it. It was equally difficult for a lower-lower class person to enter the upper-lower or lower-middle classes. Social mobility did exist, but Warner found that it was most likely to be undramatic: a person might make the step from lower-middle to upper-middle but was unlikely to leap over steps in the social ladder.

The fact that a WASP maiden lady living frugally on her inherited income in the old house on the hill might outrank socially a Russian Jewish doctor who earns four times her income probably does not seem surprising to the American reader today. However, the acceptance by Americans of the notion of social class stemmed in large part from the careful work done by Warner et al. and their followers. Other studies built on Warner's work and focused on communities in different regions of the United States to discover whether the six-class structure of Yankee City also existed in other communities. We will take a brief look at one of these studies which described a less complicated and rigid class structure than the Yankee City one.

"Plainville," the name given by James West to a midwestern town, differed from Yankee City in several ways. First, Yankee City was an older community. Second, Plainville was a farm community, while Yankee City was a manufacturing town. Third, West found two main social classes in Plainville instead of the six of Yankee City, although he noted distinctions within these two major classes. These two might be roughly characterized as the "better class" and the "lower class." They were called by West "Prairie people" and "hillbillies." West also showed that membership of an individual or group in the upper or lower class might shift, depending on the point of view of the informant. In other words, different people used different criteria to distinguish the two classes.

"Prairie people" were those who had a better farm, more modern farming technology, a long lineage in the town, more money, and more education. They tended to be open to a modern life-style in general. They described themselves as "good, honest, self-respecting, average, everyday working people," and characterized "hillbillies" as either "good, lower-class people," or "the lower element" or, at the bottom of the social scale, "people who live like animals."[2] Like Warner, West found that social distinctions were made on economic and behavioral grounds. Religion was also important, but since there were virtually no non-Protestants in Plainville, the biggest religious distinction was made between churchgoers and nonchurchgoers.

In fact, churchgoers tended to divide people into separate social groups on this basis alone. They called some "Prairie" and "hillbilly" people "good religious people." Churchgoers also called others at about the same social and economic level "good citizens, but they don't live right." On the other hand, some "lower-class" citizens talked about those higher on the social scale as "all the church hypocrites who try to keep people from making a living and having a good time."[3] But though these differences in characterization depended on a person's own position on the social ladder, there was a general agreement among Plainvillers that a two-class system existed, and that the "better class" was distinguished by church-

going, relative wealth, and a belief in "progress." However, progress was relatively new to Plainville. In 1939-40 (the time this study was made), West found Plainville to be a typical, traditional "backward" farming community, whose members looked to the not-so-distant frontier days with nostalgia for the frontier image of independence from outside interference. Old-fashioned Protestant morality, hard work, and "making it on your own" were values endorsed by Plainvillers and recognizable as part and parcel of the American Dream.

Other community studies done in the 1930s and 1940s confirmed the existence of a class system in American society and the dominance within that system of WASP Americans. Studies of Southern communities clarified group distinctions based on skin color ("race") and documented the systematic segregation of blacks and whites and the political and economic dominance enjoyed by whites.[4] However, in common with Warner when he began his studies, most Americans are uneasy with the notion of fixed social class, even though they may characterize others using class labels. And the notion of class tends to be a slippery one, difficult to define so that it can be applied to all communities or groups in America. For example, Americans are geographically mobile, so that a person might occupy an upper-class slot in their home town, but in the big city, the same person might be classified as middle class. And, as West showed, even within the same rela-

2. James West, *Plainville, U.S.A.* (New York: Columbia University Press, 1961, orig. 1945), p. 117.

3. West, *Plainville, U.S.A.*, pp. 130-31.

4. See John Dollard, *Caste and Class in a Southern Town* (New Haven: Yale University Press, 1937); Allison Davis, B. B. Gardner, and M. R. Gardner, *Deep South* (Chicago: University of Chicago Press, 1941); and Gunnar Myrdal, *An American Dilemma* (New York: Harper & Row, 1944).

tively small community, everyone does not necessarily agree upon class assignment or definitions.

However, these studies had the merit of pointing out inequalities and social differences among Americans, and of setting forth some of the ways in which people may judge themselves to be socially "higher" or "lower" than others. The community studies of social class also paved the way for recent work, often focusing on assumedly more homogeneous units—judged by the criteria of wealth, skin color, religion, ethnic background, and so forth. The concept of *subculture* has been useful here. The term subculture usually refers to a group whose members share beliefs and behaviors that in some respects differ from those of the larger or dominant culture.

Another strategy for dealing with social variety among Americans has been suggested by Spradley and McCurdy. They have suggested that since finding a bounded unit in complex society is so difficult, researchers might better look for what they call "cultural scenes," defined in the following way:

A cultural scene is the information shared by two or more people that defines some aspect of their experience. Cultural scenes are closely related to recurrent social situations. The latter are settings for action, made up of behavior and artifacts that can be observed by the outsider; the former are the definitions of these situations held by the insider.[5]

A cultural scene might be a bar, a jewelry store, a street corner, or a medical school. But the idea is not so broad as that of "subculture." Also, social scientists have used "subculture" to mean a variety of different kinds of units, sometimes defined by race, ethnicity, or age, occupation or money, or by some combination of these. However, whether we talk about subcultures or cultural scenes, there is a comparison, some-

times explicit and sometimes not, of both to the wider, more general culture. This comparison is related to the social class studies we have discussed, in that the notion of class has been expanded and redefined in an interesting manner, which will be commented on in the following paragraphs.

## "MIDDLE CLASS" AND "MAINSTREAM" CULTURE

Most social scientists and most Americans, like Warner at the beginning of his study, are uneasy with the notion of fixed social classes. Their existence contradicts the basic American belief that equality, through upward social mobility, exists in American society. Both the idea of a hereditary upper-upper class and of a constricting lower-lower class particularly challenge American ideas about equality. Ideally, they feel, there should be no permanent privileged class, nor should there be a permanent poverty-stricken class. Differences among Americans should be those that can be fitted into a middle class (which itself may be divided into several parts, lawyers being "upper"-middle and school teachers "lower"-middle). One result of this American uneasiness with the general notion of class is that for many Americans, "middle class" is often equated with "mainstream culture" or with being a "real American." It is assumed that continued prosperity has meant that more and more Americans have moved into the middle class, just as the American Dream prescribes. Thus if the middle class contains the largest number of Americans, it also must represent what "normal" Americans are like: what they want, do, and believe. Often then, when social scientists speak of subcultures, they mean non-middle-class

5. James P. Spradley and David W. McCurdy, *The Cultural Experience: Ethnography in Complex Society* (Kingsport, Tenn.: Kingsport Press, Science Research Associates, 1972), p. 24.

peoples; often too they characterize populations in terms of how close or how far they are judged to be from middle-class norms, or from mainstream culture.

But the cutoff point for middle class remains indistinct. Is a factory worker who owns his own home, makes a salary equal to that of a young executive and higher than that of a college professor to be called "working class"? Or "middle class"? Is he closer or farther from mainstream culture than the executive or the professor? Obviously, questions like these can only be answered in terms of how they relate to a specific context, to a specific group of Americans. In the following pages, we will look at some of the special definitions given of "middle class" ("mainstream") and "lower class" by different writers who have found it useful to use a two-class distinction in describing the people they worked with. We will begin by considering variations in family structure and sex role expectations among different groups of Americans.

## VARIATIONS IN FAMILY STRUCTURE AND SEX ROLES

Schneider and Smith, in their book on differences in family structure and sex roles, argue that the model of American kinship and the American family presented by Schneider in 1968 (and included in the discussion in chapter 2 of this book) applies to Americans in general at the cultural level. They feel, however, that there are important differences between what they call "middle-class" and "lower-class" norms (which provide the rules for the interaction of family members) and behavior. These writers do not define either middle class or lower class solely in socioeconomic terms. Rather, they present sets of characteristics which they label middle class or lower class.

They warn that these categories are not entirely discrete—if middle class traits were placed at one end of a scale and lower class traits at the other, most American families might place closer to the middle-class end if only one trait was considered but somewhere else if a second trait was studied. For instance, a family might be defined as lower class because the husband's job was so defined, but the norms and behavior of family members with regard to kinship might be labeled middle class.[6]

Schneider and Smith find the defining features of lower-class occupation to be the absence of mobility on the job and the absence of the possibility of continuous promotion. This definition resembles that of Berger who defined the suburbanites he studied as "working class" because they did not see upward mobility as a possibility except for their children.[7] The list of working-class jobs would include unskilled labor, service occupations, and skilled work that offers the possibility of a progression from apprentice to tradesman but no progression from tradesman to manager. Middle-class jobs are called "white collar" jobs or bureaucratic jobs. A middle-class person can expect, with luck, steady raises and promotions. Theoretically, there is no upper limit. Therefore, say Schneider and Smith, the middle-class family emphasizes planning for the future, which is expected to be more affluent than the past. The lower-class family, on the other hand, does not expect the future to be very different from the present; the emphasis is on planning for security, rather than on planning for the future.

Because the middle-class man will aspire to continuous upward mobility on the job, his worth will be judged in terms of what Schneider and Smith call "competence"—

6. David M. Schneider and Raymond T. Smith, *Class Differences and Sex Roles in American Kinship and Family Structure* (Englewood Cliffs, N.J.: Prentice-Hall, 1972).

7. Bennett M. Berger, "The Myth of Suburbia," in *Looking for America,* ed. Bennett M. Berger (Englewood Cliffs, N. J.: Prentice-Hall, 1971).

on the job and in the domain of family and kinship as well. His wife too will be judged on the basis of her competence in running the home. Competence is partially defined as being reasonable and rational, and therefore authority and decision making within the home will be delegated to whichever partner is judged most competent in any particular area. Competence for the middle-class man is supplanted by "virility" for the lower-class man, Schneider and Smith argue. The lower-class man will be judged by how "manly" he is. Similarly, in the lower-class family authority is vested in males, simply because males are seen to have a traditional right to make decisions.

The ideal of the middle-class nuclear family, say Schneider and Smith, is self-sufficiency based on an enduring solidarity between husband and wife symbolized by sexual intercourse. The concept of solidarity is extended to interests in the house, the children, and leisure activities. For the middle-class person, doing things with and for the family unit is highly stressed. However, in the lower-class family, stress is on the solidarity of the mother-child tie rather than on the husband-wife bond. In fact a husband in residence is not an essential requirement for the existence of a household. There is an expectation that households can depend for help and cooperation on a wide range of kin; the self-sufficient ideal of the middle-class nuclear family is not so stressed. Thus the boundaries of the lower-class household are more fluid. Within its structure, a variety of kin and even nonkin can be accommodated.

Further, Schneider and Smith say that within the lower-class family and kinship structure, there is a male-female split to a degree not present among the middle class. Women and men tend to have friends of their own sex with whom they interact more frequently than they do with family members of the opposite sex. Male-female relationships are seen to be less solid and enduring than female-female or male-male relationships. In addition, in opposition to the middle-class stress on doing things with and for the family as a unit, individualism within the lower class is more expected and more valued. The idea that the individual has the right to affiliate or disaffiliate with the family is accepted. A working wife, for instance, has the right to decide whether she wants to spend her money on herself or on the family. Joint checking accounts are middle class.

Thus Schneider and Smith see occupational differences in regard to the expectation of continuous promotion on the job and differences in sex-roles affecting the amount of emphasis on the husband-wife bond to be defining criteria of middle- and lower-class Americans. They say that these differences are not to be taken as absolute, or as applicable in total to any one particular family or group of families. It is clear, however, that what they sketch as middle-class norms and behavior is very close to what Schneider had defined as American culture, and that what they describe as lower class is different. While they stress that the lower-class way is just as much a coherent and structured system as the middle-class way, their picture of lower-class norms and behaviors is farther away from cultural ideals. Their formulation is general and abstract. Let us turn next to studies of specific American populations in the world of home to explore further documented variations in American kinship and family structure.

Ulf Hannerz in his book, *Soulside,* deliberately sets out to explore those ways of life in a Washington, D. C. black ghetto that *are* different from mainstream America. His definition of mainstream is shown in the following quotation:

There are people in the ghetto who have good, stable jobs, help their children with their homework, eat dinner together at a fixed hour, make payments on the car, and spend their Saturday nights watching Lawrence Welk on TV—to their largely mainstream way of life we will devote rather little attention.[8]

Aside from "mainstreamers," Hannerz labels three other life-styles which exist in the ghetto: "swingers," "street families," and "street-corner men." Here we will look at "street families" most closely because they represent a common American variation of the nuclear family ideal.

"Street families" are so named by Hannerz because much of their life is lived openly on the streets. They are child-rearing families, often headed by a woman who has usually been married, whether or not she is currently living with a husband or common-law partner. Households tend to be complex; while the "husband" slot is often not filled, the household is extended through one or more generations of women, as follows:

For example, one older woman lives with three children—two daughters, one of whom is considerably older than the other, and a son. The elder daughter has nine children, and her oldest teenage daughter in turn has a son. The older woman's other daughter has one child.[9]

This fifteen-person household is larger than most but typical in that it is extended through numerous mother-child links. It is also typical in that the women of the household are both the managers and providers, even though they may be helped from time to time by contributions from a brother, son, husband, or boyfriend. Within the home, then, women tend to have the authority. Their ex-husbands and boyfriends often are or become "street-corner" men, whose lives center around friendships maintained in drinking groups that congregate on street corners, rather than around their wives, ex-wives, or children. This kind of family has been called a "matrifocal" family by social scientists.

Hannerz believes that ghetto dwellers who live in street families are not ignorant of the mainstream model of the American family; in fact, he says, television brings this ideal to every ghetto dweller. They know that men are supposed to have steady jobs, to bring home their wages, and to assume positions of authority within the household. Yet within the ghetto about a quarter of the households do not follow this model. Hannerz sees the limited opportunities for employment success for black men as a contributing cause, since:

. . . when the man is without a job or has a kind of job generally held in low esteem throughout the society, the family may find little satisfaction in the status reflected on them. As the wife of a periodically unemployed construction worker on Winston Street puts it: 'So my husband says to me, "You ought to be happy you got a man." What's so great about being married to an old construction worker?'[10]

But he also finds that the development of a ghetto-specific kind of masculinity—the ability to talk well, to dress well, to drink liquor, to be tough, and to express concern with sexual exploits—a useful adaptation for ghetto males because it allows them to forge a "masculine" identity not dependent on holding down a good job. Women in the ghetto both disparage this ghetto image of "tough" masculinity and admire it. They expect their sons to emulate it, even though they may attempt to tell them not to drink or hang around girls. And ghetto men, while they admire the ability of women to manage the household and raise children, at times

8. Ulf Hannerz, *Soulside: Inquiries into Ghetto Culture and Community* (New York: Columbia University Press, 1969), pp. 15-16.
9. Hannerz, *Soulside:*, p. 47.
10. Hannerz, *Soulside:*, p. 74.

express a feeling that women pretend to be better than they really are. Hannerz documents some of the points made by Schneider and Smith. The street family differs markedly from the mainstream model; its boundaries are looser, its maintenance is assured by mother-child links rather than husband-wife bonds, and its norms in regard to sex-linked behavior are different. But, a child growing up in such a family will be aware of mainstream as well as ghetto-specific norms and standards.

Another documentation of variation in family structure and sex roles was presented by Herbert Gans, who studied an Italian community in Boston in the 1950s. The families Gans wrote about were not characterized by matrifocality or by frequent divorce or separation of husband and wife. Marriages tended to be more or less stable, in accord with a mainstream model. What Gans noticed, however, was that family relationships were extended along one-sex lines; that is, a man's brothers, cousins, and childhood friends formed a group. Called by Gans the "peer group," it figured prominently in social relations. Within this group, honesty, responsibility, and lack of selfishness were the ideals. A person was expected always to entertain generously, to lend money to members of his peer group. Also, within the peer group there was constant competition, expressed in new clothes, or in cars, or by lavish entertaining. Gans wrote that:

The need for display within the group is so strong among West Enders, in fact, that they find themselves unable to save because of their high expenditures of food, clothing, and other expenses of group life.[11]

Gans also found that peer-group organizations had ramifications for family structure and the attitude of men towards women and women toward men. Both husband and wife depended more on their same-sex peer group

for emotional support and for social activities than they did on each other. Gans felt that, in contrast to middle-class people, peer-group people were less adept at heterosexual relationships and viewed members of the opposite sex with suspicion. He found that in relationship to the children, the role of mother was dominant, although the father was the acknowledged head of the household.

Gans thus characterized these Italian-Americans as "person-oriented individuals," in contrast to "object-oriented individuals," whom he would classify as middle class. Richard Chalfen has shown a similar "person-oriented" versus "object-oriented" difference between groups of young black and white filmmakers. He showed each of these groups how to handle a movie camera and asked them to make a film. He found that the black youths used themselves as actors and presented dynamic situations—a party, a fight. They enjoyed presenting themselves as entertainers, as physically tough. The white youths, on the other hand, took films of sunsets, of trees and buildings, rather than of themselves or other people. They enjoyed manipulating the camera, controlling the filmmaking activity, rather than presenting themselves as actors and entertainers.[12]

However, when applied to these films, the term "person-oriented" implies a much more active view of life than that Gans said was typical of Italian peer-group members. For the Italian-American West Enders, Gans argued, individuality, particularly for males, did not exist outside the peer group. Boys, for instance, acted rough when they were with their peers but appeared passive when alone. He concluded that the predominant

11. Herbert Gans, *The Urban Villagers* (New York: The Free Press, 1962), p. 83.
12. Richard M. Chalfen, "Film as Visual Communication: A Sociovidistic Study in Filmmaking" (Ph.D. diss., University of Pennsylvania, 1974).

importance of the peer group impeded the West Enders in their attempts to fight the city's urban renewal plans. West Enders, he said, were unable to cooperate with anyone outside their peer group. They were suspicious of outsiders, of "object-oriented" people—city planners or politicians—and thus were unable to organize effectively to "fight city hall."

Both Gans and Hannerz found an emphasis on relations between people of the same sex, as predicted by Schneider and Smith, for lower-class persons, though Gans and Hannerz differ sharply in their evaluation of the specific forms of masculine behavior they noted. Hannerz felt that the companionship of males resulted in the development of a masculine image which to some extent gave ghetto men a positive self-image. This served to buffer the impossible-to-fulfill demands upon them made by mainstream ideology. Gans, on the other hand, argued that peer-group loyalty not only impeded individual growth but stymied efforts to organize effective political action. And while Gans detected "latent homosexuality" in the close relationships of the masculine peer group and in the hosility of men to women, Hannerz argued that peer groups for blacks offered an opportunity to learn the male role and to assert one's masculinity.

### FRIENDSHIP AND SOCIALIZATION ON THE STREET

Hannerz and Gans offer obviously different explanations and assessments of peer-group organization. This kind of organization—sometimes called a "gang," or "club," or a "street-corner group"—has been studied by others who wanted to understand the kinds and meanings of social relationships within a certain subculture. It has not, to my knowledge, been studied as a middle-class phenomenon, so the examples we will consider in the following paragraphs will present variations from the middle-class way to a greater or lesser extent.

William Foote Whyte's study of the Nortons, an Italian street-corner group, presents a contrast to Gans's view. Like Gans, Whyte wanted to present a picture of the social structure of the place he calls "Cornerville," but his study is more closely focused on the interaction of the members of the Nortons, a "corner-boy" club (the "boys" were young men in their late teens and early twenties). His study documents the ways in which members of the Nortons depended on each other. Like the members of Gans's peer groups, they were expected to spend money on each other, to treat each other, to help each other out. They looked for direction to their leader, Doc, whose prestige depended on his continuing generosity and willingness to put himself out for the club, even to the extent of neglecting his job.

Although the Nortons was primarily a social club whose members got together to show friendship and have fun, Whyte found that leader-follower rankings within the club existed, and the position of any one member within the club hierarchy was relatively rigid. He found, for instance, that the bowling scores of the members of the Nortons conformed exactly to their leadership or follower status within the club. Some members, although they might bowl extremely well when they bowled with non-Norton men, always lost to those who outranked them within the club. If one of these men should happen to do especially well when he was with club members, he would be subjected to kidding and verbal attack, and he would begin to do badly.

When a follower threatened to better his position . . . the boys shouted at him that he was lucky, that he was bowling over his head. The effort was made to persuade him that he should not be bowling as well as he was, that a good performance was abnormal for him.[13]

13. William Foote Whyte, *Street Corner Society*, 2d ed. (Chicago: University of Chicago Press, 1955), p. 24.

In this way the relative leader-follower position within the club was reinforced by social pressures during leisure activities.

Whyte showed that the club had a high value for the corner boys, who were reluctant to do anything that might jeopardize their friendships with club members. For this reason, corner boys were often reluctant to take a job that would require that they move out of the neighborhood. Whyte contrasted the corner-boy life-style with that of the "college boys," who were from the same neighborhood, but who expected to better their lot in life, to save money to finance their educations, and eventually to move out of Cornerville to the suburbs. For those who subscribed to the corner-boy life-style, such a move would mean giving up the all-important friendships with other corner boys; it would also mean repudiating the symbolic meaning attached to Italy and being Italian. A corner boy could achieve upward mobility without moving out of Cornerville by getting into Democratic politics or the "rackets," but, as Whyte pointed out, he then would be well known and respected in Cornerville but not outside of it in the mainstream world.

This Italian street corner group can be compared to a group of black street-corner men studied by Elliot Liebow. He showed that the men who hung out on the corner had little chance for upward mobility, even if they had been willing to forsake their old neighborhood and friends.[14] The kinds of jobs that were open to them as relatively uneducated black men led nowhere and rarely paid a living wage. Liebow felt that while these men were aware of the material and moral standards of the larger white society with which they had to deal, they also were aware that the chances for a well-paying, steady job, and a lasting relationship with a woman and with children were slight. The associations formed on the corner, then, served as a buffer against disappointments encountered on the job and at home.

The ideal for friendship relationships among corner men was a mutual supportive relationship—"going for brother"—but this ideal was often not lived up to. Compared with the Nortons, the internal organization of the street-corner group studied by Liebow was more casual. Men tended to drift in and out of the group, and the relative status of group members was not so clearly identifiable. Yet the corner served a purpose: It enabled the men to form associations which, however shaky, helped to salvage their self-respect and maintain their identities as men.

Whyte and Liebow both found that street-corner groups had a positive function for the men who participated in them. Both the Italian and black men were, in varying degrees, alienated from the social styles and values of the larger society; life on the corner, for both, gave some important rewards in the form of friendship and validation of their own worth. We can turn now to a study of somewhat younger street groups, Gerald Suttles's *The Social Order of the Slum*.[15]

Suttles's study focused on the relationships among street-corner groups, Italian, black, Mexican, and Puerto Rican, in the Addams area of Chicago. The Italians had been residents of the area for the longest period of time. Among them he found a well-defined, age-graded organization of boys' and men's groups, along with girls' and women's auxiliary groups. As a boy grew older, he would move up a hierarchical ladder until he eventually became a member of a men's political club or an "outfit" (crime-connected) organization. Similar age-graded gangs existed among the blacks,

14. Elliot Liebow, *Tally's Corner* (Boston: Little, Brown and Company, 1967).

15. Gerald D. Suttles, *The Social Order of the Slum* (Chicago: University of Chicago Press, 1968).

Mexicans, and Puerto Ricans but these were not so well established nor so rigidly organized. Suttles found that the moral and social order involved first an orderly relationship among groups, which entailed a sequence of the ways in which groups combined to fight each other or outsiders.

He outlined three levels of opposition between street-corner groups. The first and most usual involved conflict between groups of the same ethnicity but of different locality within the same age-grade—for instance, a fight between junior-grade blacks from one street with junior-grade blacks from another street. The second level of opposition involved conflict between territorial units of the same ethnic groups—for instance, blacks against Italians. The third level of conflict pulled all the residents of the Addams area together to oppose any outsiders. Suttles explained this system by referring to the social exigencies of crowded slum living. His explanation rested on the idea that people need to be able to identify people whom they can trust; these are most likely to be the people who are best known, most seen, those who live in the same block. People also need to stake out a territory which they know and in which they can feel safe. He felt, then, that conflict between groups in the slum is inevitable and necessary to maintain the social order. Conflict forces people together, he argued, and thus has a positive value. As he writes:

Individuals in the Addams area achieve a positive association with coresidents of the same age, sex, and ethnicity primarily because conflict with other persons forces them together into small face-to-face groupings. Otherwise, people might remain almost wholly isolated, associate indiscriminately, or be dependent on such dyadic relations as they could form.[16]

Here, gangs and gang fights, clearly not part of the middle-class model for bringing up children, are seen as being useful. Street-corner gangs serve the function of defining a safe and known territory populated with "people like me" who are known and therefore reliable. They thus create and promote social life, a social order.

## SUBURBIA: IS IT UNAMERICAN?

We have been talking about life "on the street," about street-corner groups and gangs which are not representative of mainstream culture, however useful they are for their members. For most Americans, the word "gang" invokes the image of a band of armed teenagers out to cause trouble to innocent people. And if they could, most Americans would move out of the city to the suburbs to protect their children from gang influences and dangers. But although Americans believe that suburbs are good places to bring up kids, suburbs have also been seen by some social scientists to present variations and even perversions of the American Dream, in a manner different from the variations of slum life.

The phenomenal growth of suburbs after World War II attracted the interest of social commentators. In the 1950s suburbs were criticized both as faulty ecological zones (places to live) and as the embodiment of a life-style seen to be inimical to old-fashioned American ideals. David Reisman in *The Lonely Crowd* stated the thesis that Americans were becoming "other-directed" instead of "inner-directed." He traced this supposed development of the American character in part to the homogenizing, conformist attitudes required by big corporations of their employees and fostered by the life-style symbolized by suburban communities.

What did Reisman and other writers mean by the life-style and attitudes of suburbanites? First, suburbs were often "de-

16. Suttles, *The Social Order*, p. 228.

velopments," that is, groups of houses designed to look more or less alike, priced within a middle-class or upper-middle-class range. The sameness of the houses and the homogeneity—in terms of age, income, and type of occupation—of the population who bought these houses were thought to create communities fundamentally different from cities. The typical suburb supposedly consisted of rows of ranch-type houses, a new modern school, and a shopping center. During the day, the suburb was seen as a woman's domain; station wagons filled with women and children made the trip from school to supermarket to dentist, while the men toiled in the city to make enough money to "keep up with the Joneses." The age, money, and occupational homogeneity was thought to result in enormous pressure for suburban dwellers to worry about being "just like" their neighbors, to keep their lawns tidy, their houses painted, and their two-car garages filled with late model cars.

Bennett Berger has suggested that this idea of the one-class, conformist suburban community is related to the idea of the melting pot. Suburbia was believed to be nonethnic and based on a visible possession of *things*—cars, a picture window, a power lawn mower, a color TV.[17] This prosperous, homogeneous community would appear to represent the logical outcome of the melting process. Yet critics saw the suburb as a perversion of American ideals in that the values of individualism and independence, the insistence on acting according to the dictates of conscience and not according to the dictates of one's neighbors, had disappeared. It was thought that people who moved to suburbs almost automatically joined numbers of voluntary organizations, started going to church for social rather than religious reasons, and became registered Republicans. In other words, the new suburbanite was believed to shed his or her old life-style, ethnic identity, and individualism and to

assume the posture of a stereotypic and materialistic middle-class American.

Sloan Wilson's novel, *The Man in the Gray Flannel Suit,* presents such a picture of suburbia and its emphasis on material possessions rather than moral decisions. The hero of the book, a junior executive, worries that his marriage will dissolve because his wife has found out about his wartime affair in Italy. But basically, he is more concerned about money. Miraculously, his personal problems disappear, and a happy ending is in sight when an inheritance materializes. The conformist aspect of suburbia is present in another book, a study of Park Forest, Illinois, by William H. Whyte. In Park Forest the construction of the houses and apartments around a central court meant that no family had privacy. Consequently, group pressure was extreme, said Whyte; neighborliness was felt to be the prime virtue. Instead of trying to buy things in order to get ahead of their neighbors, Park Forest people were constrained *not* to buy things until the group decided the purchase was all right. Otherwise, people would be accused of being ostentatious or of trying to be "better" than others. Conformity to the norms of the community was expected and desired.[18]

These two books contributed to the view that suburbia was conformist, middle class, and stifling of individuality or creativity. However, later studies showed that suburbs are not all this homogeneous or this middle class. Berger's *Working Class Suburb* described a community inhabited by industrial workers who did *not* automatically become churchgoing, organization-joining Republicans when they moved out of the

---

17. Bennett M. Berger, "Suburbs, Subcultures and Styles of Life," *Looking for America,* pp. 165-187.

18. William H. Whyte, Jr., *The Organization Man* (New York: Doubleday, 1957); Sloan Wilson, *The Man in the Gray Flannel Suit* (New York: Simon and Schuster, 1955).

city. Nor did becoming homeowners make them automatically middle class.[19] His findings have been reinforced by Dobriner's discussion of three different kinds of suburbs and by Gans's study of Levittown, New Jersey.[20]

Dobriner compared a relatively new suburb with an older one and also with a rural community undergoing "suburbanization" against its will. He concluded that each presented a different slice of American life and that the differences among them could best be described by social class variables. Gans found that the Levittowners' basic life-styles were *not* changed by the move to the suburbs. For instance, kinship ties were not necessarily broken, and aspirations for and definitions of "the good life" changed very little. In other words, as Warner had pointed out, differences or likenesses among people in American society cannot be entirely explained by differences in income, the ability to buy a house as the prime example here. Variation continues to exist even in lookalike places like suburbs. The melting pot hypothesis, however attractive, does not hold.

## PUBLIC SCHOOL AND OTHER INSTITUTIONS

So far we have been talking about variations in family structure, sex role expectations, and socialization patterns outside the home. We will turn now to a discussion of other institutions to see some of the ways in which they may differ from the idealism expressed in the American belief system. We will begin by summarizing some of the remarks Erving Goffman has made with regard to what he named "total institutions." While we are not going to discuss total institutions in detail here, Goffman's insight into the effects of institutions on persons, his recognition that they represent a new culture to which the individual must adapt, has led anthropologists and others to consider seriously the relationship of individuals to other, less "total" institutions in society—among them, the public school.

Goffman defined as "total institutions" those which take over every aspect of a person's life. These include jails, mental hospitals, orphanages, army barracks, ships, convents, and boarding schools, among others. Goffman writes that the encompassing or total character of these institutions is symbolized by real physical barriers—locked doors, barbed wire, high cliffs—which seal the institution off from the rest of the world. By describing life in a mental institution, he showed that the experience of being mentally ill was in large measure determined by the need for the patient in a mental hospital to adjust to the special culture of the institution itself. A person who adjusted well, who learned the rules quickly and was willing to conform to them, would be judged less ill than a patient who was unable to learn to adjust or who rebelled. Thus the judgment by doctors and attendants of a patient's relative sickness depended to a great extent on whether or not the patient knew how to behave, rather than on the state of the patient's mind.

Goffman noticed that total institutions have various features in common—for instance, degradation or initiation procedures which ensured that the newly arrived inmate must forsake his or her status on the outside and must learn a new status and new rules for behavior to get along on the inside. The better the prisoner, the boarding school pupil, or the mental patient learns how to adapt to the institutional environment, the more chance of success he or she will have. Success means staying out of trouble and, in the case of the convict or

19. Bennett M. Berger, *Working Class Suburb* (Berkeley: University of California Press, 1960).
20. Herbert J. Gans, *The Levittowners* (New York: Random House, 1967); William M. Dobriner, *Class in Suburbia* (Englewood Cliffs, N. J.: Prentice-Hall, 1963).

mental patient, getting out of the institution.[21]

In many ways, Goffman's observations apply also to public schools in America, even though their institutional scope is not total. Kheif, for instance, has suggested that one way to look at schools is to compare them to other institutions in American culture, even jails:

As for what is prison-like about the school, in some upper-middle-class schools, children—because of over-crowded facilities—cannot talk while eating their 15-minute lunch: because of the rule of silence, they develop an elaborate nonverbal system of communication as if they were inmates of a prison or a Tibetan convent. Some slum schools are run as if they were day jails: maximum security is enforced constantly by teachers, principal and school counselors.[22]

Other writers have noted ways in which schools treat pupils as if they were "nonpersons" or inmates, incapable of running their own lives. In the early school years, conforming to rules is reinforced by the practice of assigning grades for behavior as well as for academic subjects—"gets along well with others," "respects the property of others," and similar categories are employed. Learning "right" behavior is often judged explicitly by the teacher as being just as important as learning to read. One fourth-grade teacher, for instance, spent hours getting her students to memorize the following verse, to be recited "with expression":

> By your actions you are showing
> You know how to climb the stairs,
> When you *look* where you are going,
> And walk singly, not in pairs.

In some schools, even fully grown adolescents are required to obtain a hall pass from the teacher in order to go to the lavatory.

Policing the halls becomes a large part of the teachers' and administrators' jobs.

It has been suggested that because of this police function of American schools, American children continue to act like nonresponsible people long after they have grown up; either they must conform to nonsensical rules and regulations, or they must rebel, become "troublemakers" and, eventually, "drop outs." Edgar Friedenberg, author of *Coming of Age in America* is one writer who had shown concern over the conformity of attitude and behavior he found in the public schools.

In his study based on interviews with twenty-five students in each of nine high schools in different parts of the country, he found that qualities like popularity, good manners, and conformity to group standards were highly valued by the students. To his dismay, he found that "being different," whether that meant being unusually intelligent, talented, or original, or whether it meant being of a different social status than the majority of students, was not admired by students. They tended to think that people who were different were weird. They also showed a respect for, or at least a willingness to go along with, whatever standards of thought and behavior were considered normal by their peers and by their teachers and other authority figures.

Friedenberg also found that at most high schools children whose family backgrounds were less privileged almost always suffered from the preconceptions of their teachers about poor children, black children, or any other children who did not fit the teachers' idea of a neat middle-class model. His book voices a double complaint. First, he says schools serve to hammer children into sub-

21. Erving Goffman, *Asylums* (Garden City, N.Y.: Anchor Books, Doubleday, 1961).
22. Bud B. Kheif, "The School as a Small Society," in *To See Ourselves*, ed. Thomas Weaver (Glenview, Ill.: Scott, Foresman and Co., 1973), p. 284.

mission. While Americans intend that schools should socialize their children, make them into "good Americans," most believe this socialization should not force their children to become carbon copies of each other. Second, Friedenberg notes that those children who are not considered malleable, or who refuse to mold themselves acceptably, do not even gain the dubious achievement of the docile majority. He finds "equal opportunity" is not as a rule present in American schools.

Therefore he concludes that schools fail on two major counts: first, because they do not encourage creative and original thinking; and, second, because they cannot even teach the fundamentals of reading, writing, and job acquisition skills to a sizeable minority of Americans. His view is expressed by the following quotation:

Basically, then, I disapprove of compulsory school attendance in itself. I see no valid moral reasons to single out the young for this special legal encumbrance. A people have no right to cling to arrangements that can be made halfway workable only by imposing an infantile and unproductive status on adolescents and indoctrinating them with a need for trashy goods and shallow, meretricious relationships that they know to be degrading. There are social reasons, too; the family has lost many of its functions through adaptation to social change and now has no more place for its young than any other social institution has and no real basis for dealing with them. If the children were not in school, many parents would go mad; and the schools, for all their defects, are more orderly and safer places, with a little more care and better food, than many homes.[23]

Thus Friedenberg, though he is highly critical of the ways American high schools operate, realizes that schools pick up where families leave off in socializing the young person to take part in the world of work.

As he points out, schools exist in part because they give some relief to parents from the constant task of caring for their young, perhaps a special burden in a nuclear family where there are only two adults responsible for the children. Friedenberg stresses that schools teach young people to conform and not to think. He notes too that social inequalities based on differences in skin color or on other criteria are exaggerated by the differential treatment given some children in school. The social system of the school mirrors the wider social system; schools, he finds, do not serve as melting pots which obliterate social differences, nor do they reward only individual achievement.

The picture of the school as a more-or-less self-serving institution is reinforced by Harry Wolcott's ethnography of the life of an elementary school principal. This study is concerned with how much time the principal spends in each activity, how he handles authority, and how his personality and talents become an influence in the school. Wolcott concludes that the primary role of an elementary school principal is to serve as mediator—between teachers and pupils, between parents and the school, and between his own school and the school board. He acts to make sure that the system continues to run as smoothly as possible; he is not an innovator or a real educator.

The principal's actions, like his pupils', are dictated more by what is happening around him than by what he himself might want to do. In fact, he is run by the school, rather than the other way around. There is a reminder, again, of Goffman's observations on the nature of a person's actions in an institutional setting. The actions of an attendant in a mental ward could be characterized in the same way that Wolcott de-

23. Edgar Z. Friedenberg, *Coming of Age in America: Growth and Acquiescence* (New York: Vintage Books, 1965, orig. 1963), p. 249.

scribes the duties of the principal.[24] We can see then, both from the point of view of the pupils and of the administrators, that American public school does not necessarily fit neatly with American beliefs concerning equality of opportunity and rugged individualism.

## WORKING AND NOT WORKING

We can turn now to the world of work to answer a series of questions. To what degree are American ideas about the value of work realized on the job? What about the notion that a person should work to get ahead, to achieve upward mobility? How is work defined? How are people who don't work categorized? We will begin by considering this last question, by referring to a study of a retirement community.

Just as new material possessions are valued in America, so are young, "new" people, particularly those who work. In 1945, James West wrote about the traditional farming community of Plainville:

The word 'old' means different things to Plainvillers of different ages, but in the eyes of people in the prime of life, rearing families and participating actively in the community's social and economic institutions, a married couple begins to be considered 'old' when one of the pair can no longer do his or her work. People who cannot work are quickly considered as belonging 'on the shelf.'[25]

In 1974 an ethnography of a community for people "on the shelf," *Fun City*, written by Jerry Jacobs, shows that American attitudes toward being old and not working have apparently changed very little in almost thirty years[26]

Fun City is a planned development for retired people. It is not really a suburb, since it is geographically isolated and is self-sufficient; there is no travel by its residents to and from the city. While house prices

are in the middle range, the residents have come from various occupational backgrounds. What they have in common is their relative age and their enforced leisure.

Although there are a myriad of voluntary activities open to the residents of Fun City, Jacobs found that most of the residents did not participate in them or in fact in many social activities at all. Particularly as they grew older, and perhaps ill and unable to drive a car, they found themselves more and more isolated. Thus although the lure of Fun City was that it was intended to be stress-free—no crime, no pollution, no crowding, no work obligations—yet many residents found it a false paradise. Those people who were most pleased with their lives in Fun City, Jacobs found, were those who were successful in making work for themselves—putting on dramatic performances, transcribing books into braille, collecting clothes for the needy in other communities, or serving as volunteers in a nearby hospital. As he writes:

All these activities can be viewed as attempts by residents to make their leisure-time activities meaningful and legitimate, that is, to introduce aspects of work into their leisure-time pursuits in much the same way as leisure was formerly introduced into the routine of work.[27]

He suggests that although people may be attracted to places like Fun City because it is supposedly conflict-free, a conflict-free environment is in many ways unnatural, certainly not what these people had been used to. And since Americans believe that a per-

24. Harry F. Wolcott, *The Man in the Principal's Office* (New York: Holt, Rinehart and Winston, 1973).

25. West, *Plainville, U.S.A.*, p. 203.

26. Jerry Jacobs, *Fun City: An Ethnographic Study of a Retirement Community* (New York: Holt, Rinehart and Winston, 1974).

27. Jacobs, *Fun City:*, p. 77.

son's value is measured in terms of work, the older people themselves feel they have lost their sense of being worthwhile. For many residents then, the Fun City environment reinforces their feeling that they lack personal value. Being in Fun City means that they are literally isolated from society, as if they were in cold storage. Jacobs feels that the retirement community becomes not only unnatural and unhuman, but inhumane.

When we turn to a study about people whose community is defined by their work, the contrast is startling. Longshoremen in Portland are the subject of this book by Pilcher, who studied them as a community united through the longshoremen's union and its hiring hall. Here they must congregate if they want to work; here they associate with other longshoremen who are often kin or close friends.

Pilcher traces the source of the longshoremen's unity by detailing the history of the union. The union provides them with a common background and a common myth which dates from the bloody struggles of the 1930s, in particular the strike of 1934, out of which the union was formed. Pilcher summarizes the effects of the strike in the following way:

The effect of the strike on the longshoremen was very similar to that of a successful revolutionary war on a people: it gave a sense of having engaged in important historical processes and working together toward a common goal. There was a fair amount of actual physical violence during the strike and the tales of the battles grow somewhat more important and more magnificent in each telling, and the principal figures in some of these have almost the stature of George Washington and John Paul Jones. Indeed, all of these legends have become welded together into one great origin myth. In the beginning, the employer ruled supreme and all longshoremen were little more than slaves, but under the leadership of Harry Bridges the nobler of the longshoremen arose in righteous wrath, demolished the power of the employer, and delivered their fellow workers from onerous servitude and humiliation.[28]

Pilcher's observations of the life of longshoremen represent an ethnography of the world of work exclusively. This world is totally masculine, in fact and in ideology. Longshoring is dangerous and difficult physical work, performed only by males. Further, in the work setting certain kinds of language use involving different classes of profanity and swearing are used to alleviate the tension and to create solidarity among work group members. This kind of language is not felt to be appropriate in front of women, nor is other "rough and tough" behavior associated with longshoremen, which they are proud to claim as part of their masculine image. One can compare the proud masculinity of the longshoremen at work to the enforced make-work of the residents of Fun City, who engage in unpaid volunteer activities of the type usually relegated to middle-aged, middle-class women.

The contrast between the longshoremen and the Fun City residents is evident also as Pilcher outlines the longshoremen's belief system. He finds that longshoremen value personal independence, individualism, and the freedom from a rigid work schedule given them by longshoring. While they make good wages and even take extra "moonlighting" jobs in order to live well, they were little interested in upward mobility, that is, in more prestige or a higher status in society. Rather, they were proud of being longshoremen and proud that none of them had to submit to the rigid and impersonal schedule imposed by an assembly line factory job. Pilcher felt that they typified the "frontier mentality" which is so much a part of the American ideology.

28. William W. Pilcher, *The Portland Longshoremen* (New York: Holt, Rinehart and Winston, 1972), p. 115.

The identity of longshoremen is part and parcel of their work, and, in this respect, they seem typically American. Now we will look at the lives of people who, either willingly or against their better judgment, are defined by the fact that they are not working and, unlike Fun City residents, are not retired workers. These are the tramps studied by James Spradley. Spradley subtitled his book *Urban Nomads;* part of the definition of being a tramp is having no permanent home, being forced to worry each night about a warm and dry place to sleep. Part of the definition of a tramp also involves drinking in public and being picked up by the police and, because tramps rarely have money, serving some time in jail.

Here we are talking about a social category rather than a community based on occupation, like longshoring. Being a tramp involves a certain kind of behavior that is in general disapproved of by most Americans. The label "tramp" is given to a person by outsiders who judge his behavior to be deviant from accepted norms. Acceptance of this label by the urban nomads, Spradley found, differs among tramps. There are those who have fully accommodated themselves to being a tramp for the rest of their lives. But there are others who see their nomadic way of life as temporary, who are not yet willing to accept the deviant label.

Pilcher found that many of the older longshoremen had "seen the world" by riding the boxcars in their youth. For them, traveling this way was a cheap method of seeking adventure and did not result in the adoption of nomadism as a permanent way of life. Free travel also fit in with the longshoreman's image of himself as an independent and self-sufficient adventurer, and thus represented for him what Pilcher would characterize as the frontier, pioneering spirit. But though not all of them felt themselves miserable and some did value their independent, footloose life, Spradley's tramps

characterized themselves and were seen by society as being at the bottom of the social heap, the dregs of Skid Row.[29] Spradley argues that these men are penalized by society—labeled deviant, forced to spend time in jail—simply because they do not conform to an American notion of correct middle-class behavior.

The tramp, by his way of life, appears to have rejected middle-class norms and values and this may be a greater threat than criminal violence.[30]

We might suggest also that, in the case of the tramp, not working and not looking for work may be his single most deviant act.

Working, especially on an assembly line, is not, as many Americans know, always such a source of pride and masculine identity as it is for longshoremen. Donald Roy has shown the ways in which the assembly line can be humanized and the tedious job made bearable in his article, "Banana Time."[31] The day in the cutting room at the factory where Roy worked with three other men was broken up by "times"—periods of ritual social interaction. "Lunch time" was only one of these; there were others, not formally labeled by the workers, but called by Roy "peach time," "banana time," and "window time." These had grown out of the association of the men with each other and were unique to this work group. "Peach time," for instance, was announced by Sammy, who every day would share peaches with the others, who always complained about the

---

29. James P. Spradley, *You Owe Yourself a Drunk* (Boston: Little, Brown and Company, 1970), p. 262.
30. Spradley, *You Owe Yourself a Drunk*, p. 105.
31. Donald F. Roy, "Banana Time: Job Satisfaction and Informal Interaction," in *Anthropology and American Life*, eds. Jorgensen and Truzzi (Englewood Cliffs, N. J.: Prentice-Hall, 1974), pp. 323-47.

quality of the fruit but always accepted it. "Banana time," on the other hand, was announced by Ike who would sneak a banana from Sammy's lunch box and eat it himself. These "times" were accompanied by constant jokes and discussion which always centered around the same topics. The importance of the structured "times" and joking was made clear one day when Roy tried to change slightly the usual half-insults made about one man's in-laws. His attempt resulted in the breakdown of the group social system. For thirteen days, all social intercourse stopped, the work situation again became devoid of human content and unbearably boring. The exchange of fruit and insults was thus shown to be absolutely necessary in order to maintain a livable work atmosphere.

We have not yet looked at the definition of work and have in fact discussed only men's work. One instructive variant of the American definition of work was shown in a study centered on Mexican-American children done by Mary Ellen Goodman and Alma Beman. These children, aged 7-13, were interviewed to find out the ways in which they viewed the boundaries of their community and how they saw their family and school. Of interest here is the slightly unusual definition of work these children gave. Their definition included more than the job the man of the house does for a wage. The children classified their sister's care of younger siblings as "work" too. As Goodman and Beman write:

In an industrial world's definition, work is closely allied with the acquisition of things and status. But for the most of these children, whether they are describing careers or tasks at home, the stress is not on the activity itself, nor on the personal achievement. It is, rather, on the contribution made. In the family everybody works in his own way: this is part of living, like enjoying family meals, watching a tele-vision show, or playing with other family members.[32]

This is not to say that for these children the "outside" world of work and the "inside" world of home are not separate; they remain so. But work is considered to be done on the "inside" as well; the definition is expanded to include all activities which contribute to the welfare of the household, rather than just those which bring in money.

**CONCLUSION**

This review of some of the literature on American society is far from exhaustive or complete; any student of America will realize far more was left out than included. We have tried to indicate, however, some of the documented variety of American life. Not all Americans live in nuclear families, for instance. Not all nuclear families are self-sufficient or wish to be so. Variations in the ways in which children or young people are socialized—in gangs or on street corners—do not always conform to American ideals. Further, ethnic, racial, or class distinctions are apparently not disappearing. Suburbs, like cities, are not necessarily the real-life counterpart of melting pot ideology.

In addition, American institutions like the public school sometimes appear more like jails than educational institutions: the American Dream values often seem to be lost or perverted during the educational process. And while most Americans do accept work as a measure of their value to society, not all regard it as the one road to salvation, and not all aspire to higher social status. There are indications that the concept of work may be understood differently by

32. Mary Ellen Goodman and Alma Beman, "Child's-Eye Views of Life in an Urban Barrio," in Jorgensen and Truzzi, *Anthropology and American Life*, p. 153.

different groups of Americans. It would appear that no matter how small the group or institution under study, Americans usually do not conform in their behavior to the core American beliefs set out in chapters 1 and 2.

So having documented differences among Americans, let us turn to a new examination of the meaning of the American Dream in reality. How do Americans deal with the problems of diversity and conformity? How are the tensions between the belief in equality and the belief in individual achievement resolved for Americans? What happens when non-WASP Americans are confronted with the incongruence of their unique subcultural practices and understandings with the accepted WASP standards? How do Americans understand and cope with the fact that American society remains heterogeneous and that social inequality exists? In chapter 4, we will look at these questions and at some of the answers that have been suggested to the American puzzle.

### For Further Reading

Howell, Joseph T. *Hard Living on Clay Street: Portraits of Blue Collar Families.* Garden City, N. Y.: Doubleday Anchor Books, 1973. A sympathetic account of two Southern white families living in Washington, D. C.

Jorgensen, Joseph G. and Marcello Truzzi, eds. *Anthopology and American Life.* Englewood Cliffs, N. J.: Prentice-Hall, 1974. A collection of anthropological articles on various aspects of American life.

Kammeyer, Kenneth C. W., ed. *Confronting the Issues: Sex Roles, Marriage and the Family.* Boston: Allyn and Bacon, Inc., 1975. A collection dealing with contemporary opin-

ions on the changing American family, sex roles, and sexual practices.

Labov, William. *Language in the Inner City: Studies in the Black English Vernacular.* Philadelphia: University of Pennsylvania Press, 1972. A serious analysis of the grammatical rules used in the black English vernacular which helps explain difficulties in communication between black students and white teachers.

Seeley, J. R., R. A. Sim and E. W. Loosely. *Crestwood Heights: A Study of the Culture of Suburban Life.* New York: John Wiley and Sons, 1963 (orig. 1956). An excellent study of a Canadian suburb.

Warner, W. Lloyd. *American Life: Dream and Reality,* rev. ed. Chicago: University of Chicago Press, 1962. A good summary of much of the material presented by Warner in earlier works.

Worth, Sol and John Adair. *Through Navajo Eyes: An Exploration in Film Communication and Anthropology.* Bloomington: Indiana University Press, 1971. A discussion which analysis of films made by Navajo filmmakers.

### Bibliography

Berger, Bennett M. 1971. *Looking for America.* Englewood Cliffs, N. J.: Prentice-Hall.

Friedenberg, Edgar Z. 1965 (orig. 1963). *Coming of Age in America: Growth and Acquiescence.* New York: Vintage Books.

Hannerz, Ulf. 1969. *Soulside: Inquiries into Ghetto Culture and Community.* New York: Columbia University Press.

Reisman, David. 1950. *The Lonely Crowd: A Study of the Changing American Character.* New Haven, Conn.: Yale University Press.

Warner, W. Lloyd, ed. 1963. *Yankee City,* rev. ed. in 1 vol. New Haven, Conn.: Yale University Press.

# 4 | Dream and Reality

In the preceding chapter the studies we looked at showed diversity in American society, variations on American themes. It appears that practically all Americans are in some ways different and thus not mainstream. For some large groups, the promises of the American Dream are never kept.

The fact that inequalities between groups in American society exist and persist is often hard for Americans to accept. While they recognize that some individuals will be more successful than others, acceptance of social inequality among groups is more difficult. Individual differences in social status are implied by the premises of the American belief system, which stress the value of the individual and the worth of hard work and achievement. But the discovery that equal opportunity for mobility is constrained by the factors of relative wealth, skin color, sex, or religion often represents for Americans a brutal shock. As Potter wrote:

Social barriers in this country are a violation of our national ideas, and therefore the mere awareness of them impairs public morale. Whereas other societies accept them as part of the order of nature, we have refused to recognize them and have conducted life on the theory that they do not exist. Hence our people are not prepared to encounter them and are less able psychologically to adjust to them,

with the result that, when such barriers do force themselves upon public notice, many people either lose confidence in themselves or rebel against the society which, as they feel, betrayed them with a false promise.[1]

In the 1960s and 1970s many Americans were forced to realize for the first time that flagrant and deep-seated social inequalities exist in American society. Many reacted to this unwelcome knowledge with rebellion or disgust. Yet most continue to believe that rational solutions to social problems can be found, that human ingenuity can overcome all difficulties.

In this chapter we will look briefly at some of the kinds of inequalities that have been brought to the attention of Americans in the past decade. We will try to understand how these inequalities between groups are related to the American belief system. We will then turn our attention to American thinking about solutions to social problems.

## POVERTY AND RACISM

Distinctions between rich and poor and between white and nonwhite Americans are

1. David M. Potter, *People of Plenty* (University of Chicago Press, 1954), p. 101.

not the only social differences that persist in America, but they remain the most perplexing and the most obvious. Why, in the richest country in the world, should there be groups of people who are not adequately fed or housed? And why, in a country whose citizens profess a belief in equality under the law, should social distinctions be made on the basis of the color of a person's skin? We can't hope to answer these questions fully, but we can look at some ways in which poverty and racism are related to American beliefs in general.

American thinking about poverty has been influenced by the belief in the morality of hard work, and the belief that equality of opportunity inevitably will provide the chance for a decent job and at least moderate success for all people. Therefore, Americans reason, if a person is really poor it must be because he or she does not work hard enough, or worse, does not want to work.

This view, of course, ignores reality. Many people with very low incomes are physically handicapped and unable to work. Others are old and unable to work, in some cases because they are required to retire, to leave their jobs, at some specified age. Further, many people work steadily at jobs which simply do not pay a living wage. As Edwin Eames and Judith Goode write:

One fact that continually surprises analysts is that a large proportion of the poor are employed on a full-time basis.[2]

Eames and Goode also point out that there are many kinds of marginal jobs, such as construction work, which are seasonal and thus insecure. Ill-paid or seasonal jobs, along with illegal activities like "hustling" (prostitution), are, in urban America, the opportunities that are available to people who lack the requisite education or skill or perhaps the union contacts to obtain better work. This group of Americans is often made up of people who have most recently moved from rural areas into the cities. Their agricultural knowledge and skills and their physical strength are not useful in the new environment. They become the poor, or lower class.

We have noted before the tendency of social scientists and Americans in general to think of "American" as being middle class, or mainstream. The belief system sketched in chapter 1 of this book and labeled the Amercan Dream could today be seen as a definition of middle-class values. As Conrad Arensberg and Arthur Niehoff explain:

There is still a national core, usually characterized as that of the middle class, having its origins in Western European culture. . . . It seems justifiable to characterize the middle class value system of the United States, as derived originally from Europe but modified to suit local conditions, as the core of American culture.[3]

But if we consider middle-class values to represent the core of American culture, are we to consider non-middle-class people, by definition including the poor, to be less solidly American? Christopher Jencks writes:

If words are to mean anything at all, we have to call a prosperous doctor's family "upper-middle class" even if the parents have reduced all their children to autism. Conversely, we have to call an impoverished laundry worker's family "working class" or "lower class," even if all the children have IQs of over 180 and

2. Edwin Eames and Judith Cranich Goode, *Urban Poverty in a Cross-Cultural Context* (New York: The Free Press, 1973), p. 223.

3. Conrad M. Arensberg and Arthur H. Niehoff, "American Cultural Values," in *The Nacirema*, eds. James P. Spradley and Michael A. Rynkiewich (Boston: Little, Brown and Company, 1975), p. 364.

have earned graduate degrees from exclusive universities.[4]

Obviously, in some sense he is right. Yet it would be hard to call the laundry worker's family un-American or nonmainstream American simply because they are impoverished and by definition not middle class. In fact the laundry worker's family embody American ideals and values—hard work, education, and upward mobility.

This example is brought up to show some of the confusion in American thinking about poverty, work, being middle class, and being American. If we use the terms "middle class" and "lower class" to refer to different income levels or educational attainments, the terms may be useful to describe differences in social status. But if we mean when we call a person lower class that this person does not share fully in the system of American cultural beliefs, we can easily be wrong. More important, we may be expressing a judgment that lower-class people, being poor, are less worthy and less truly American than middle-class ones.

We can understand that American negative judgments about the poor are related to and are a consequence of the beliefs in the morality of hard work and the necessity for independence and self-relance. Further, relative poverty for some people is a logical consequence of the American economic system. In a society which rewards the individual who can succeed in competition for the best-paying job, not everyone can win. But how can we understand the ideology behind racism in America? How can Americans deny equality and the chance to compete freely to groups of people whose skins are of a different color?

Social inequalities based on skin color most certainly have complex causes. Thus the queston raised above cannot hope to be answered fully in this book. Instead, we will look at the ways in which two anthro-

pologists have attempted to relate the fact of racism to the American belief system.

The first writer is Louis Dumont, a Frenchman who has written extensively on the caste system in India and has compared it to the color barrier in America. Dumont argues that recognition of social differences based on skin color follows logically from the American belief in equality when seen in the context of the European background of American culture. He points out that western European tradition was based on the idea of a matter-versus-spirit and soul-versus-body split. Americans affirm that all souls are equal. Logically then, they locate differences in the *body*, that is, in physical attributes like skin color. Dumont's argument, essentially, is that if one believes that all men are created equal, then those who are *obviously* created different, having darker skins, must be a class of people *less* equal. Further, he notes that:

It is as if only physical characteristics were essentially collective where everything mental tends to be primarily individual.[5]

Dumont thus bases his argument on the logical but paradoxical entailments of American beliefs in equality. Frances Hsu, on the other hand, suggests that the dominant American value is that of self-reliance. The self-reliant individual, he says, is basically insecure and is easily threatened.

In his continuous effort at status achieving and maintenance, the self-reliant man fears nothing more than contamination by fellow human beings who are deemed inferior to him. This contamination can come about in diverse forms: sharing the same desks at the same schools,

4. Christopher Jencks et al., *Inequality* (New York: Harper & Row, 1972), p. 78.
5. Louis Dumont, *Homo Hierarchicus* (Chicago: University of Chicago Press, 1970), p. 255.

being dwellers of the same apartments, worshipping in the same churches, sitting in the same clubs, or being in any situation of free and equal contact.[6]

This fear of contamination, of losing one's place on the status ladder, leads many Americans to behave in ways that are opposite to the ideal they have been taught. They will act aggressively against people who are felt to threaten security or upward mobility.

Hsu's explanation rests on psychological assumptions related to the American value of self-reliance. He seeks to explain discrimination of all kinds. Dumont traces the logic of the American belief in equality and advances an explanation for the existence of discrimination based on skin color specifically. Both writers acknowledge the reality of racism in America, however, and both relate it to core American values. While Hannerz has shown that the life-styles of ghetto blacks in America represent logical social systems which allow blacks to construct for themselves a meaningful life, he does not argue that discrimination is nonexistent nor that life for black ghetto dwellers is not often harsh and difficult. Opportunities for black Americans and especially for poor black Americans are limited. Discriminatory policy and belief combined with negative moral judgments of poverty produce and perpetuate social inequalities.

However, even when confronted with the existence of obvious social inequalities like poverty and racism, most Americans continue to believe in and hope for the ultimate realization of the American Dream. Inequalities in society are seen as problems to be met and vanquished. Americans feel, for instance, that the real reason that the war on poverty of the 1960s was not won was because the necessary money and knowledge were lacking. Given time, Americans believe, rationality will triumph, solutions will be found.

## SOLUTIONS: EQUALITY VERSUS INDIVIDUALISM

Not surprisingly, there is controversy over plans for solutions to social problems, just as there is argument over what constitutes ideal American society. Reisman and Friedenberg in their examinations of suburbs, big corporations, and public schools found that the doctrine of equality often meant, in real social situations, the loss of individuality and creativity. Reisman called the conforming person "outer-directed" to indicate that the person was ruled by social pressure and not by his or her conscience. The corporation man was seen as less worthy than the self-reliant and independent pioneer, and unlike George Washington, was assumed to be able to tell a lie to get along or get ahead. Friedenberg also deplored conformity among high school students—"getting along," being popular, not causing trouble, fitting in.

But though Friedenberg disliked conformity, he was also disturbed that nonwhite high school students were not learning the skills that would enable them successfully to conform. They remained different, outside the mainstream. And in general, Americans and American social scientists have felt that the life-styles or social fates of people who are too "different" present problems. For instance, the life-style of the urban poor has been called "alienated," "pleasure seeking," "hard-living," and even "culturally deprived." (The term 'culturally deprived' literally makes no sense in anthropological terms, of course. All human beings share in a culture and must do so, if they are to survive. The phrase "culturally deprived" really means something like "not sharing in *my* culture," or simply "different from me.")

6. Frances L. K. Hsu, "American Core Value and National Character," in *The Nacirema*, eds. James P. Spradley and Michael A. Rynkiewich (Boston: Little, Brown and Company, 1975), p. 388.

The dilemma presented by the tension between two prominent values—equality on one hand and individualism on the other—would seem to be the core of the American puzzle. One question is, how is mediocrity to be avoided if equality is to be achieved? And the converse of the first question is, if differences among groups of people persist, how can the ideal of equality be realized?

The tension between the values of equality and individualism is not new, of course. And in the past there have been many changes in law and custom which have occurred in response to new social needs and new perceptions of the discrepancy between the ideology and the reality. One important change has been the expansion of the meaning of phrases like "We, the people of the United States . . ." in the preamble to the U.S. Constitution. In the eighteenth century, "we, the people" referred to white males. In fact many of the Founding Fathers felt that the rights and duties of citizenship should be restricted to white male property owners, the group felt to be rational enough to vote and to take an active part in framing the laws and electing the leaders of the country. Gradually, the meaning of "we, the people" changed and broadened to include poor Americans, blacks, American Indians, women, and most recently, Americans who are eighteen years old. Practices which prevented some classes of people from exercising their right to vote —poll taxes or literacy tests—have gradually been abolished.

We can look at the change in thinking and practice in regard to public education as well. Originally, the public school system was not intended to provide an extensive education for all. Reading and writing were judged adequate knowledge for most people. But faced with floods of non-English speaking immigrants in the late nineteenth century, the school system expanded and evolved. It became an instrument of socialization. The melting pot ideology was born. In this century Americans have accepted the idea that all people should have access to a university education too. This policy has led to "open admission" in some state universities: it is accepted that a person has a right to as much learning as he or she is capable of. Further, the emphasis on the practical aspects of education, begun in the public schools in order to teach children the American way, has also resulted in curriculum changes in universities. No longer does a liberal education necessarily require years of training in Latin and Greek. And one may earn an advanced degree in practical arts like forestry or social work.

The expansion of university education is particularly interesting because it was largely motivated by the belief that implementation of the doctrine of "equal opportunity" could modify the extent of social inequalities. The argument holds that if every individual is given a chance to vote and to go to college, then any inequalities will be traceable to individual differences in ability and effort. The doctrine of equal opportunity has also been applied in the work world. Employers are required by law to hire individuals who are qualified for jobs without regard for their color or sex, for example. The idea is to give the poor or the nonwhite or female person access to the same educational facilities and to the same job opportunities as the middle-class white person. This approach to solving basic inequalities in society has been the motivation behind other recent social policy, like school desegregation. It is one of the two major approaches which have been implemented in recent years.

The other basic approach, as Eames and Goode remark, tries to modify the behavior of the poor or nonwhite person so that they will no longer act or be seen as "different." Many governmental programs have combined the two approaches:

Job training programs which can be seen as modifiyng behavior by "correcting" attitudes to dress, time and language also intervene in the opportunity structure when they train skills and place those whom they have trained in jobs. However, many educational programs emphasize resocialization and broadening experience to "compensate" for deprivation; such programs proceed on the assumption that the system is one of equal and adequate opportunity.[7]

In regard to these two basic ideas about how to solve inequalities in America, we can again see the opposition of the values of equality and individualism. Plans which emphasize the broadening of opportunities for the individual continue to encourage and reward individual success and effort. Plans which hope to teach non-middle-class people how to be more like the middle class are, in effect, attempts to soften individual differences so that people will conform to the prevailing standards. The equal-opportunity approach implies an acceptance of the possibility of individual differences, but a denial that enduring distinctions and inequalities among groups persist. Resocialization plans, on the other hand, imply that being different from mainstream America is less worthy than being conformist: in a sense, this approach can be seen as the reworking in twentieth-century terms of the melting pot ideology. However, it has become clear that many nonmainstream Americans have no real desire to be just like the white middle-class majority. The slogan "black is beautiful" expresses a pride in a distinct heritage and identity, as does this statement, made by a Mexican-American Texan:

I'm proud of being an American, but I won't become a gringo (a white, or Anglo-American). Now they're offering us equality. That's fine. I want to be equal before the law and have a chance to make money if I choose. But the Anglos are denying me the right to be myself. They want me to be like them. I want the chance to be a Mexican-American and to be proud of that Mexican bit. The Anglos offer us equality, but whatever happened to freedom?[8]

It is clear that neither equal opportunity nor resocialization programs, although both have had some success, are the ultimate answer to the problem posed by social inequalities in America. Americans continue to believe in the ideal of equality and at the same time in the ideal of the independent frontiersman. The contradiction between these ideals remains, and in America as in other cultures, tensions between ideals and reality will continue to exist. Yet Americans also maintain a belief in rational solutions to all problems: new solutions will be proposed.

## CONCLUSION

In attempting to understand American culture from the anthropological point of view, we become aware of the implicit assumptions which are shared by Americans. We can offer no solutions to the American puzzle as yet. The goal remains to continue to try to see the culture as a whole, to research problems and direct interest towards groups of people about which we know far less than we assume. Generally, we assume that we know what "middle class" means, for instance. But as I have tried to show, this label is at best a shorthand way of summing up social and economic factors, and at worst, it supplies social scientists and others with a moral yardstick, the supposed living out of the American Dream by a largely mythical population. The closer we get to actual life-styles and behaviors, the less it seems that any Amer-

7. Eames and Goode, *Urban Poverty*, p. 231.
8. Quoted by William Madsen, *The Mexican-Americans of South Texas*, 2nd ed. (New York: Holt Rinehart and Winston, 1973), p. 16.

ican population really embodies American cultural ideals.

However, an approach to problems of inequality in America can be guided by an understanding of the American belief system. Further, we can propose that given the complexity of American society homogeneity is neither to be expected nor desired. The melting pot myth served to help change many institutions, to promote the idea of equal opportunity and to extend the scope of civil rights. Yet it is clearly not true. The problems of diversity and inequality continue to face Americans and can perhaps be better dealt with if acknowledged. A recent interview between Gregory Bateson, an anthropologist, and Stewart Brand, editor of the *Whole Earth Catalogue*, illustrates this final point:

Bateson: There are two forms of colonial administration. There is that form of colonial administration which says that the natives have got to be like the colonists. This is missionary endeavor, all that, and becomes a tyranny. The other form of colonial administration says that the natives have got to be like themselves and had better not change. "They have such a beautiful sense of rhythm." Then poetry freezes and everything dies and the flowers can't make seed and nothing goes. So neither of these will do. To do either becomes imperialism.
Brand: I ask how you choose, then.
Bateson: (Slowly.) The truth which is important is not a truth of preference, it's a truth of complexity . . . of a total eco-interactive ongoing web. . . .
Brand: Relationship without preference works how?
Bateson: Only preference for its complexity.[9]

You will notice that this book, like that of any other American writing about America, ends with a moral.

**For Further Reading**

Brand, Stewart. *II Cybernetic Frontiers*. New York: Random House and Berkeley: The Bookworks, 1974. Includes the interview with Bateson mentioned in the text, as well as a fascinating discussion of computer games and the people who play them.

Eames, Edwin, and Judith Goode. *Urban Poverty in a Cross-Cultural Context*. New York: The Free Press, 1973. See the chapter on poverty in urban American for a lucid and critical look at theory and policy and the poor.

Novak, Michael. *The Rise of the Unmeltable Ethnics*. New York: Macmillan, 1972. An argument for the right of white ethnic minorities to retain their unique cultural values.

Spradley, James P. and Michael A. Rynkiewich, eds. *The Nacirema*. Boston: Little, Brown and Company, 1975. A useful and interesting collection of articles on America, including many classic pieces.

**Bibliography**

Eames, Edwin and Judith C. Goode. 1973. *Urban Poverty in a Cross-Cultural Context*. New York: The Free Press.

Dumont, Louis. 1970. *Homo Hierarchicus*. Chicago: University of Chicago Press.

Jencks, Christopher. 1972. *Inequality*. New York: Harper & Row.

Spradley, James P. and Michael A. Rynkiewich, eds. 1975. *The Nacirema*. Boston: Little, Brown and Company.

9. Stewart Brand, "Both Sides of the Necessary Paradox: Conversations with Gregory Bateson," in *II Cybernetic Frontiers* (New York: Random House and Berkeley: The Bookworks, February, 1974), p. 33.

# *Glossary*

**Affines**—Relatives by marriage; in-laws.

**Age-Grade**—A social category defined by age, e.g., teenagers.

**Bilateral Descent**—The rule that allows people in America to count as kin all persons who are geneologically related through both males and females.

**Culture**—(1) A learned set of beliefs and understandings about the meanings of people. (2) The opposite of nature: that order in society created by human beings.

**Extended Family**—A kinship group composed of two or more nuclear families affiliated through an extension of the parent-child or sibling relationship.

**Homogamy**—Marriage with one's equal; the unstated rule that a spouse should be selected from that group of people who are of the same age, race, religion, ethnicity, education, and wealth.

**Incest Rule**—A prohibition of sexual intercourse (and marriage) between certain specified relatives.

**Mainstream Culture**—That American culture which is judged typical of the average American; middle-class culture.

**Matrifocal Family**—A kinship group whose primary and most stable members are female.

**Nature**—(1) The logical opposite of culture: i.e., not created by humans. (2) In America, human nature: thus culture is considered to be natural because it is the product of human rationality.

**Neolocal Residence**—The establishment by a newly married couple of a residence of their own separate from that of the bride's or groom's family.

**Norms**—Rules which specify behavior which society labels desirable; may be written or unwritten.

**Nuclear Family**—A two-generation kinship group consisting of a married couple and their unmarried children.

**Siblings**—People who are the children of the same mother and father; brothers and sisters.

**Social Class**—A group in society defined by the criteria of income, education, occupation, etc., as being more or less prestigious than other such groups.

**Socialization**—The process by which a human being learns to be a functioning member of his or her culture.

**Street-Corner Groups**—Male social groups whose interaction takes place primarily in public, on the street.

**Subculture**—A group within a culture whose members share beliefs and behaviors that in some respects are different from those of the larger culture.

**Symbol**—An object, sound, or gesture which arbitarily represents activities or beliefs.

**Total Institution**—An institution which is separated from the larger society so that its members must learn the institutional culture created.

# Index

abundance, vii, 5, 9, 21-22
advertising, 21-22
age-grades, 22
American Dream, 9-10, 24, 38, 45-46, 52
Arensberg, Conrad M., 48

bald eagles:
   preservation of, 6
Bateson, Gregory, 53
Beman, Alma, 45
Berger, Bennett, 38-39
Beverly, Robert, 6
Brand, Stewart, 53

cities:
   ambivalence toward, 7-8
cleanliness, vii, 21

Declaration of Independence, 1-2, 10
democracy, 4, 8, 12
Dobriner, William M., 39
Dumont, Louis, 2, 49

Eames, Edwin, 48, 51
Emerson, Ralph Waldo, 9-10
equality, 2, 6, 8:
   and conformity, 40-41, 52

family and kinship, 14-15, 33-34
Franklin, Benjamin, 2
Friedenberg, Edgar Z., 40-41, 50
frontier:
   influence of, 5

Gans, Herbert, 34-35, 39
Goffman, Erving, 39-40
Goode, Judith, 48, 51
Goodman, Mary Ellen, 45

Hannerz, Ulf, 32-35
Henry, Jules, 15, 21-22
Hsu, Frances, 49

individualism, 5, 43, 52
inequality, 27-30, 25, 40-41, 47-53
Iroquois, 1-2

Jacobs, Jerry, 42-43
Jefferson, Thomas, 8
Jencks, Christopher, 24, 48, 49

Kennedy, John F., 17
Kheif, Bud B., 24, 40

Liebow, Eliot, 20, 36

mainstream culture. *See* middle class.
marriage, 15, 16, 18, 23
Mather, Cotton, 11
Mead, Margaret, 25
melting pot, 12-13, 24, 38-39, 51
middle class, 30-32, 38, 48, 49, 52
moral judgements, 3-4, 10, 18

Niehoff, Arthur H., 48

Pilcher, William W., 43-44
Potter, David M., 6, 10, 47
poverty, 10, 47-50
Price, Richard, 7
progress, 6, 8-9, 21, 23
Protestant ethic, 11

race and racism, 28, 47-50
rationality, 2, 3, 8

retirement community, 42-43
Roy, Donald F., 44-45

Schneider, David M., 15, 16, 23, 31
schools, 15, 23-26, 39-40, 41, 51
sex-roles, 19, 20, 31-32, 33, 35, 43
Smith, Raymond T., 31-32
social class, 27-30, 49, 52
Spradley, James P., 30, 44
street corner groups, 34-37
subculture, 30-36, 44, 45
suburbs, 37-40
success. *See* progress, upward mobility.
Suttles, Gerald D., 36

technology, 6-8
Turner, Frederick Jackson, 5, 19

upward mobility, 9, 24, 28, 31, 36
U.S. Constitution, 1, 3, 4, 51

Warner, W. Lloyd, 27-30, 39
Washington, George, 24, 25
West, James, 28-30, 43
Whyte, William Foote, 35, 36
Whyte, William H., Jr., 38-39
Wolcott, Harry, 41-42
work world, 15, 20, 42-45